To:

From:

Date:

The
EVERYDAY
Prayer
MAP®
JOURNAL
for Women

**DEVOTIONAL INSPIRATION
PLUS PRAYER MAPS**

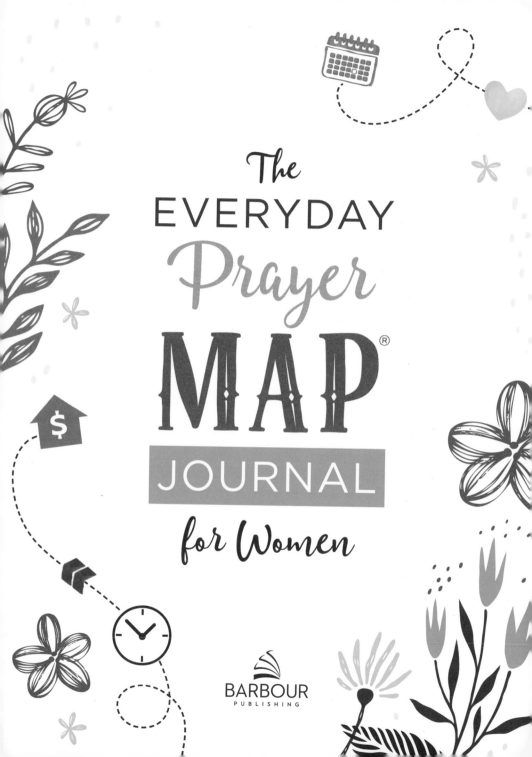

The EVERYDAY Prayer MAP® JOURNAL for Women

BARBOUR
PUBLISHING

Member of the
Evangelical Christian
Publishers Association

Printed in China.

INTRODUCTION

Barbour's The Prayer Map journals are perennial bestsellers, with more than half a million copies sold. This brand-new *The Everyday Prayer Map Journal for Women* provides you with page after page of guided "maps" to follow as you talk to God about things that matter most to your heart. Whether you're experiencing anxiety, grief, fear, stress, hopelessness, hardship, or something more, this journal is overflowing with daily, practical, purposeful prayer maps to help you more fully experience the life-changing power of prayer in your life. Throughout this journal, you'll be prompted to create your very own Prayer Maps (already outlined in a colorful design), resulting in helpful guides for your personal prayer time. You can follow your Prayer Maps—from start to finish!—as you talk to God each day.

Each map includes a spot to record the date, so you can look back on your prayers and see how God has listened, loved, and answered. *The Everyday Prayer Map Journal for Women* will help you build a healthy spiritual habit of continual prayer for life!

Sections Include:

Section 1:
When You Just Need to Talk to God

BE THE BRIDGE

"I looked for someone among them who would build up the wall and stand before me in the gap on behalf of the land so I would not have to destroy it, but I found no one."
EZEKIEL 22:30 NIV

Each prayer request you offer up to God is important to you, and when you ask others to pray, you're counting on them to help carry you through the tough times.

Do you give the same consideration to those who ask you for prayer? It's easy in the busyness of life to overlook a request someone else has made. Maybe you don't know the person very well or you don't really understand what he or she is going through. Perhaps the request came in a text that you quickly glanced at and then deleted. Yet even with texted prayer requests, others trust you to stand in the gap for them during difficult times in their lives.

Don't delay. Take time right when you receive a request to talk to the Lord on the requester's behalf. Be the bridge that carries that person through the valley of darkness back to the mountaintop of joy.

Heavenly Father, help me to have a heart of compassion for those I know and even for those I don't know who need Your comfort and love. Help me never to be too busy to pray for them. Amen.

Date:

Dear Heavenly Father, ...
....
....
....
....
....

Thank You for...
....
....
....
....
....
....
....
....
....

People I am praying for today...
....
....
....
....
....
....
....
....

I am worried about...
....
....
....
....

Here's what's happening in my life. . .

....

....

....

....

I need. . .

....

....

....

....

....

Other things on my heart that I need to
share with You, God. . .

....

....

....

....

....

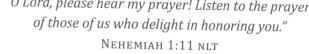

Thank You, Father, for hearing my prayers. *Amen.*

*"O Lord, please hear my prayer! Listen to the prayers
of those of us who delight in honoring you."*
NEHEMIAH 1:11 NLT

Date:

Dear Heavenly Father, ...
....
....
....
....
....

Thank You for...
....
....
....
....
....
....
....
....

People I am praying for today...
....
....
....
....
....
....
....
....
....
....

I am worried about...
....
....
....
....

Here's what's happening in my life. . .

I need. . .

Other things on my heart that I need to
share with You, God. . .

Thank You, Father, for hearing my prayers. _Amen._

*The earnest prayer of a righteous person has great
power and produces wonderful results.*
JAMES 5:16 NLT

Date:

Dear Heavenly Father, ...
....
....
....
....
....

Thank You for...
....
....
....
....
....
....
....
....

People I am praying for today...
....
....
....
....
....
....
....
....
....

I am worried about...
....
....
....
....

Here's what's happening in my life. . .

....
....
....
....
....

I need. . .

....
....
....
....
....
....

Other things on my heart that I need to share with You, God. . .

....
....
....
....
....

Thank You, Father, for hearing my prayers. *Amen.*

*Listen to my cry for help, my King and
my God, for I pray to no one but you.*
PSALM 5:2 NLT

Date:

Dear Heavenly Father, ...
....
....
....
....
....

Thank You for...

....
....
....
....
....
....
....
....

People I am praying for today...

....
....
....
....
....
....
....
....
....

I am worried about...

....
....
....
....

Here's what's happening in my life. . .

I need. . .

Other things on my heart that I need to share with You, God. . .

Thank You, Father, for hearing my prayers. *Amen.*

Pray that the Lord's message will spread rapidly and be honored wherever it goes.
2 Thessalonians 3:1 nlt

Date:

Dear Heavenly Father, ...

....

....

....

....

Thank You for. . .

....

....

....

....

....

....

....

People I am praying for today. . .

....

....

....

....

....

....

....

I am worried about. . .

....

....

....

....

Here's what's happening in my life. . .

_____
_____
_____
_____

I need. . .

_____
_____
_____
_____
_____

Other things on my heart that I need to share with You, God. . .

_____
_____
_____
_____
_____

Thank You, Father, for hearing my prayers. *Amen.*

"Keep on asking, and you will receive what you ask for. Keep on seeking, and you will find. Keep on knocking, and the door will be opened to you."
Matthew 7:7 nlt

Date:

Dear Heavenly Father, ...
....
....
....
....
....

Thank You for. . .
....
....
....
....
....
....
....
....

People I am praying for today. . .
....
....
....
....
....
....
....
....
....

I am worried about. . .
....
....
....
....
....

Here's what's happening in my life. . .

_____
_____
_____
_____

I need. . .

....
....
....
....
....

Other things on my heart that I need to
share with You, God. . .

....
....
....
....
....

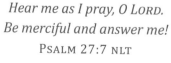

Thank You, Father, for hearing my prayers. *Amen.*

Hear me as I pray, O LORD.
Be merciful and answer me!
PSALM 27:7 NLT

Date:

Dear Heavenly Father,

Thank You for...

People I am praying for today...

I am worried about...

Here's what's happening in my life. . .

_____
_____
_____
_____

I need. . .

_____
_____
_____
_____
_____

Other things on my heart that I need to share with You, God. . .

_____
_____
_____
_____
_____

Thank You, Father, for hearing my prayers. *Amen.*

Devote yourselves to prayer with an alert
mind and a thankful heart.
COLOSSIANS 4:2 NLT

Date:

Dear Heavenly Father, ...
....
....
....
....
....

Thank You for. . .

....
....
....
....
....
....
....
....

People I am praying for today. . .

....
....
....
....
....
....
....
....
....

I am worried about. . .

....
....
....
....
....

Here's what's happening in my life. . .

I need. . .

Other things on my heart that I need to share with You, God. . .

Thank You, Father, for hearing my prayers. *Amen.*

"O Lord, you are a great and awesome God! You always fulfill your covenant and keep your promises of unfailing love to those who love you and obey your commands."
DANIEL 9:4 NLT

Date:

Dear Heavenly Father, ...
....
....
....
....
....

Thank You for. . .
....
....
....
....
....
....
....
....
....

People I am praying for today. . .
....
....
....
....
....
....
....
....
....

I am worried about. . .
....
....
....
....
....

Here's what's happening in my life. . .

_____

_____

_____

_____

I need. . . _____

_____

_____

_____

_____

_____

Other things on my heart that I need to
share with You, God. . .

_____

_____

_____

_____

_____

Thank You, Father, for hearing my prayers. *Amen.*

But each day the LORD pours his unfailing love
upon me, and through each night I sing his
songs, praying to God who gives me life.
PSALM 42:8 NLT

Date:

Dear Heavenly Father, ...
....
....
....
....
....

Thank You for...
....
....
....
....
....
....
....
....

People I am praying for today...
....
....
....
....
....
....
....
....
....

I am worried about...
....
....
....
....
....

28

Here's what's happening in my life. . .

I need. . .

Other things on my heart that I need to
share with You, God. . .

Thank You, Father, for hearing my prayers. *Amen.*

*I pray that God, the source of hope, will fill you completely
with joy and peace because you trust in him.*
Romans 15:13 NLT

Date:

Dear Heavenly Father,

Thank You for...

People I am praying for today...

I am worried about...

Here's what's happening in my life. . .

_____

_____

_____

_____

I need. . .

_____

_____

_____

_____

_____

Other things on my heart that I need to share with You, God. . .

_____

_____

_____

_____

_____

Thank You, Father, for hearing my prayers. *Amen.*

"Pray with all your might!
And don't let up!"
1 SAMUEL 7:8 MSG

Date:

Dear Heavenly Father, ...
....
....
....
....
....

Thank You for...
....
....
....
....
....
....
....
....

People I am praying for today...
....
....
....
....
....
....
....
....
....

I am worried about...
....
....
....
....
....

Here's what's happening in my life. . .

I need. . .

Other things on my heart that I need to share with You, God. . .

Thank You, Father, for hearing my prayers. *Amen.*

We always pray for you, and we give thanks to God, the Father of our Lord Jesus Christ.
COLOSSIANS 1:3 NLT

Date:

Dear Heavenly Father, ...
....
....
....
....
....

Thank You for...

....
....
....
....
....
....
....
....

People I am praying for today...

....
....
....
....
....
....
....
....

I am worried about...

....
....
....
....
....

Here's what's happening in my life. . .

....
....
....
....

I need. . .
....
....
....
....
....

Other things on my heart that I need to
share with You, God. . .

....
....
....
....
....

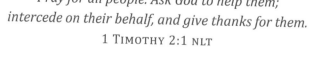

Thank You, Father, for hearing my prayers. *Amen.*

Pray for all people. Ask God to help them;
intercede on their behalf, and give thanks for them.
1 TIMOTHY 2:1 NLT

Date:

Dear Heavenly Father, ...
....
....
....
....
....

Thank You for...
....
....
....
....
....
....
....
....

People I am praying for today...
....
....
....
....
....
....
....
....
....

I am worried about...
....
....
....
....

Here's what's happening in my life. . .

I need. . .

Other things on my heart that I need to share with You, God. . .

Thank You, Father, for hearing my prayers. *Amen.*

Answer my prayers, O LORD,
for your unfailing love is wonderful.
PSALM 69:16 NLT

Date:

Dear Heavenly Father, ...
....
....
....
....
....

Thank You for...
....
....
....
....
....
....
....
....
....

People I am praying for today...
....
....
....
....
....
....
....
....
....

I am worried about...
....
....
....
....
....

Here's what's happening in my life. . .

I need. . .

Other things on my heart that I need to share with You, God. . .

Thank You, Father, for hearing my prayers. *Amen.*

They will pray for you with deep affection because of the overflowing grace God has given to you.
2 CORINTHIANS 9:14 NLT

Date:

Dear Heavenly Father, ...
....
....
....
....
....

Thank You for...

....
....
....
....
....
....
....
....

People I am praying for today...

....
....
....
....
....
....
....
....

I am worried about...

....
....
....
....

Here's what's happening in my life. . .

_____
_____
_____
_____

I need. . .

_____
_____
_____
_____
_____
_____

Other things on my heart that I need to
share with You, God. . .

_____
_____
_____
_____
_____

Thank You, Father, for hearing my prayers. *Amen.*

Because he bends down to listen,
I will pray as long as I have breath!
PSALM 116:2 NLT

Date:

Dear Heavenly Father, ...
....
....
....
....
....

Thank You for. . .
....
....
....
....
....
....
....
....
....
....

People I am praying for today. . .
....
....
....
....
....
....
....
....
....

I am worried about. . .
....
....
....
....
....

Here's what's happening in my life. . .

....
....
....
....

I need. . .

....
....
....
....
....
....

Other things on my heart that I need to share with You, God. . .

....
....
....
....
....

Thank You, Father, for hearing my prayers. *Amen.*

I pray that from his glorious, unlimited resources he will empower you with inner strength through his Spirit.
EPHESIANS 3:16 NLT

Date:

Dear Heavenly Father, ...
....
....
....
....
....

Thank You for. . .
....
....
....
....
....
....
....
....
....

People I am praying for today. . .
....
....
....
....
....
....
....
....
....

I am worried about. . .
....
....
....
....
....

Here's what's happening in my life. . .

....

....

....

....

I need. . . ....

....

....

....

....

....

Other things on my heart that I need to
share with You, God. . .

....

....

....

....

....

Thank You, Father, for hearing my prayers. *Amen.*

God's way of putting people right shows up in the acts of faith,
confirming what Scripture has said all along: "The person
in right standing before God by trusting him really lives."
ROMANS 1:17 MSG

Date:

Dear Heavenly Father, ...
....
....
....
....
....

Thank You for...
....
....
....
....
....
....
....
....

People I am praying for today...
....
....
....
....
....
....
....
....
....

I am worried about...
....
....
....
....
....

Here's what's happening in my life. . .

_____
_____
_____
_____

I need. . .

_____
_____
_____
_____
_____

Other things on my heart that I need to
share with You, God. . .

_____
_____
_____
_____
_____

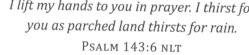

Thank You, Father, for hearing my prayers. *Amen.*

I lift my hands to you in prayer. I thirst for
you as parched land thirsts for rain.
PSALM 143:6 NLT

Date:

Dear Heavenly Father, ...
....
....
....
....
....

Thank You for...
....
....
....
....
....
....
....
....
....

People I am praying for today...
....
....
....
....
....
....
....
....
....
....

I am worried about...
....
....
....
....

Here's what's happening in my life. . .

....

....

....

....

I need. . .

....

....

....

....

....

Other things on my heart that I need to share with You, God. . .

....

....

....

....

....

Thank You, Father, for hearing my prayers. *Amen.*

"Bless those who curse you.
Pray for those who hurt you."
LUKE 6:28 NLT

49

Date:

Dear Heavenly Father,

Thank You for...

People I am praying for today...

I am worried about...

50

Here's what's happening in my life. . .

....

....

....

....

I need. . .

....

....

....

....

....

Other things on my heart that I need to
share with You, God. . .

....

....

....

....

....

Thank You, Father, for hearing my prayers. *Amen.*

*I pray that your love will overflow more and more, and that
you will keep on growing in knowledge and understanding.*
PHILIPPIANS 1:9 NLT

Date:

Dear Heavenly Father,..
....
....
....
....
....

Thank You for...
....
....
....
....
....
....
....
....
....
....

People I am praying for today...
....
....
....
....
....
....
....
....
....

I am worried about...
....
....
....
....
....

Here's what's happening in my life. . .

_____

_____

_____

_____

I need. . .

_____

_____

_____

_____

Other things on my heart that I need to share with You, God. . .

_____

_____

_____

_____

_____

Thank You, Father, for hearing my prayers. *Amen.*

"Love your enemies! Pray for those who persecute you!"
MATTHEW 5:44 NLT

Date:

Dear Heavenly Father, ...
....
....
....
....

Thank You for...
....
....
....
....
....
....
....
....

People I am praying for today...
....
....
....
....
....
....
....
....
....

I am worried about...
....
....
....
....

Here's what's happening in my life. . .

....

....

....

....

I need. . .

....

....

....

....

....

Other things on my heart that I need to
share with You, God. . .

....

....

....

....

....

Thank You, Father, for hearing my prayers. *Amen.*

*I also pray that you will understand the incredible
greatness of God's power for us who believe him.*
EPHESIANS 1:19 NLT

Date:

Dear Heavenly Father, ...
....
....
....
....

Thank You for. . .
....
....
....
....
....
....
....
....
....

People I am praying for today. . .
....
....
....
....
....
....
....
....
....

I am worried about. . .
....
....
....
....
....

Here's what's happening in my life. . .

I need. . .

Other things on my heart that I need to share with You, God. . .

Thank You, Father, for hearing my prayers. *Amen.*

I pray to you, O LORD, my rock.
PSALM 28:1 NLT

Date:

Dear Heavenly Father, ...
....
....
....
....
....

Thank You for...
....
....
....
....
....
....
....
....
....

People I am praying for today...
....
....
....
....
....
....
....
....
....

I am worried about...
....
....
....
....
....

Here's what's happening in my life. . .

....

....

....

....

I need. . .

....

....

....

....

....

Other things on my heart that I need to
share with You, God. . .

....

....

....

....

....

Thank You, Father, for hearing my prayers. *Amen.*

*"You can pray for anything, and if you
have faith, you will receive it."*
MATTHEW 21:22 NLT

59

Date:

Dear Heavenly Father, ...
....
....
....
....
....

Thank You for...

....
....
....
....
....
....
....
....

People I am praying for today...

....
....
....
....
....
....
....
....
....

I am worried about...

....
....
....
....

Here's what's happening in my life. . .

....

....

....

....

I need. . .

....

....

....

....

....

Other things on my heart that I need to
share with You, God. . .

....

....

....

....

....

Thank You, Father, for hearing my prayers. *Amen.*

*In your unfailing love, O God, answer my
prayer with your sure salvation.*
PSALM 69:13 NLT

Section 2:
When You're Afraid

FEER-FREE

You will not fear the terror of night,
nor the arrow that flies by day.
PSALM 91:5 NIV

Were you afraid of the dark when you were a little girl? It's hard to be comfortable when you can't see what's out there, right? Even as a big girl, the nighttime hours can still be a little scary. Seems like we're most vulnerable to fears and failures in the wee hours, when the darkness closes in around us.

So, how do you face the "terror of night" without fear? You have to grasp the reality that God is bigger and greater than anything that might evoke fear. He's bigger than financial struggles. He's bigger than job stress. He's even bigger than relational problems. Best of all, He can see in the dark. He knows what's out there and can deal with it. All it takes is one sentence from Him: *"Let there be light!"* and darkness dispels.

We serve an awesome and mighty God, one who longs to convince us He's mighty enough to save us, even when the darkness seeps in around us. So don't fear what you can't see. Or what you *can* see. Hand over that fear and watch God-ordained faith rise up in its place.

Father, I'm glad You can see in the dark. Sometimes I face the unseen things of my life with fear gripping my heart. I release that fear to You today. Thank You for replacing it with godly courage.

DATE:

Dear Heavenly Father, ...
....
....
....
....

Today I am afraid. . .
....
....
....
....
....
....
....
....
....

(and I'm giving ALL my fears to You!)

I need Your strength and courage in these areas of my life. . .
....
....
....
....
....
....
....
....
....
....
....
....

64

I need Your help focusing my thoughts on. . .

....

....

instead of

....

....

I need Your comfort. . .

....

....

....

....

I am so thankful for all the ways You love and care for me, including. . .

....

....

....

....

Thank You, Father, for hearing my prayers. *Amen.*

This is My command: be strong and courageous.
Never be afraid or discouraged because I am
your God, the Eternal One, and I will
remain with you wherever you go.
Joshua 1:9 voice

65

DATE:

Dear Heavenly Father,

Today I am afraid. . .

(and I'm giving ALL my
fears to You!)

I need Your strength
and courage in these
areas of my life. . .

66

I need Your help focusing my thoughts on. . .

....

....

instead of

....

....

I need Your comfort. . .

....

....

....

....

I am so thankful for all the ways You love and care for me, including. . .

....

....

....

....

Thank You, Father, for hearing my prayers. *Amen.*

"Be strong. Take courage. Don't be intimidated. . . .
Because GOD, your God, is striding ahead of you. He's right
there with you. He won't let you down; he won't leave you."
DEUTERONOMY 31:6 MSG

DATE:

Dear Heavenly Father, ...
....
....
....
....
....

Today I am afraid. . .
....
....
....
....
....
....
....
....
....
....

(and I'm giving ALL my
fears to You!)

I need Your strength
and courage in these
areas of my life. . .
....
....
....
....
....
....
....
....
....
....
....

I need Your help focusing my thoughts on. . .

....

....

instead of

....

....

I need Your comfort. . ....

....

....

....

....

I am so thankful for all the ways You
love and care for me, including. . .

....

....

....

....

Thank You, Father, for hearing my prayers. *Amen.*

*Fear not, be not dismayed, for the Lord God, my God, is with
you. He will not fail or forsake you until you have finished
all the work for the service of the house of the Lord.*
1 Chronicles 28:20 ampc

DATE:

Dear Heavenly Father,

Today I am afraid. . .

(and I'm giving ALL my
fears to You!)

I need Your strength
and courage in these
areas of my life. . .

I need Your help focusing my thoughts on. . .

....

....

instead of

....

....

I need Your comfort. . .

....

....

....

....

I am so thankful for all the ways You love and care for me, including. . .

....

....

....

....

Thank You, Father, for hearing my prayers. *Amen.*

Be brave. Be strong. Don't give up.
Expect GOD to get here soon.
PSALM 31:24 MSG

DATE:

Dear Heavenly Father,

Today I am afraid. . .

(and I'm giving ALL my fears to You!)

I need Your strength and courage in these areas of my life. . .

I need Your help focusing my thoughts on. . .

....

....

instead of

....

....

I need Your comfort. . .

....

....

....

....

I am so thankful for all the ways You love and care for me, including. . .

....

....

....

....

Thank You, Father, for hearing my prayers. *Amen.*

*They will not live in fear or dread of what may come,
for their hearts are firm, ever secure in their faith.*
PSALM 112:7 TPT

Dear Heavenly Father,

Today I am afraid. . .

(and I'm giving ALL my
fears to You!)

I need Your strength
and courage in these
areas of my life. . .

I need Your help focusing my thoughts on. . .

....

....

instead of

....

....

I need Your comfort. . .

....

....

....

....

I am so thankful for all the ways You love and care for me, including. . .

....

....

....

....

Thank You, Father, for hearing my prayers. *Amen.*

Fear not [there is nothing to fear], for I am with you; do not look around you in terror and be dismayed, for I am your God. I will strengthen and harden you to difficulties, yes, I will help you; yes, I will hold you up and retain you with My [victorious] right hand of rightness and justice.
ISAIAH 41:10 AMPC

DATE:

Dear Heavenly Father, ...
....
....
....
....
....

Today I am afraid. . .
....
....
....
....
....
....
....
....
....
....

(and I'm giving ALL my
fears to You!)

I need Your strength
and courage in these
areas of my life. . .
....
....
....
....
....
....
....
....
....
....
....
....
....

I need Your help focusing my thoughts on. . .

....

....

instead of

....

....

I need Your comfort. . .

....

....

....

....

I am so thankful for all the ways You love and care for me, including. . .

....

....

....

....

Thank You, Father, for hearing my prayers. *Amen.*

Don't be paralyzed in any way by what your opponents are doing. Your steadfast faith in the face of opposition is a sign that they are doomed and that you have been graced with God's salvation.
PHILIPPIANS 1:28 VOICE

DATE:

Dear Heavenly Father,
....
....
....
....
....
....

Today I am afraid. . .
....
....
....
....
....
....
....
....
....
....

(and I'm giving ALL my
fears to You!)

I need Your strength
and courage in these
areas of my life. . .
....
....
....
....
....
....
....
....
....
....
....
....

I need Your help focusing my thoughts on. . .

....

....

instead of

....

....

I need Your comfort. . .

....

....

....

....

I am so thankful for all the ways You
love and care for me, including. . .

....

....

....

....

Thank You, Father, for hearing my prayers. *Amen.*

*Be strong and of good courage. Dread not
and fear not; be not dismayed.*
1 Chronicles 22:13 ampc

DATE: _____

Dear Heavenly Father, _____
_____
_____
_____
_____
_____

Today I am afraid. . .
_____
_____
_____
_____
_____
_____
_____
_____
_____

(and I'm giving ALL my
fears to You!)

I need Your strength
and courage in these
areas of my life. . .
_____
_____
_____
_____
_____
_____
_____
_____
_____
_____
_____
_____

I need Your help focusing my thoughts on. . .

....

....

instead of

....

....

I need Your comfort. . .

....

....

....

....

I am so thankful for all the ways You love and care for me, including. . .

....

....

....

....

Thank You, Father, for hearing my prayers. *Amen.*

"Behold—God is my salvation! I am confident,
unafraid, and I will trust in you."
Isaiah 12:2 TPT

81

DATE:

Dear Heavenly Father,

Today I am afraid. . .

(and I'm giving ALL my fears to You!)

I need Your strength and courage in these areas of my life. . .

82

I need Your help focusing my thoughts on. . .

....

....

instead of

....

....

I need Your comfort. . .

....

....

....

....

I am so thankful for all the ways You
love and care for me, including. . .

....

....

....

....

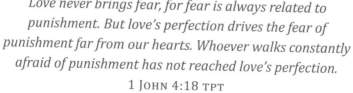

Thank You, Father, for hearing my prayers. *Amen.*

Love never brings fear, for fear is always related to
punishment. But love's perfection drives the fear of
punishment far from our hearts. Whoever walks constantly
afraid of punishment has not reached love's perfection.
1 JOHN 4:18 TPT

DATE: _____

Dear Heavenly Father, ...
....
....
....
....
....

Today I am afraid. . .
....
....
....
....
....
....
....
....
....
....

(and I'm giving ALL my fears to You!)

I need Your strength and courage in these areas of my life. . .
....
....
....
....
....
....
....
....
....
....
....
....

I need Your help focusing my thoughts on. . .

....

....

instead of

....

....

I need Your comfort. . .

....

....

....

....

I am so thankful for all the ways You love and care for me, including. . .

....

....

....

....

Thank You, Father, for hearing my prayers. *Amen.*

No need to panic over alarms or surprises, or predictions that doomsday's just around the corner, because GOD will be right there with you; he'll keep you safe and sound.
PROVERBS 3:25–26 MSG

85

DATE:

Dear Heavenly Father,
....
....
....
....
....
....

Today I am afraid. . .
....
....
....
....
....
....
....
....
....
....
....

(and I'm giving ALL my
fears to You!)

I need Your strength
and courage in these
areas of my life. . .
....
....
....
....
....
....
....
....
....
....
....
....
....
....

I need Your help focusing my thoughts on. . .

....

....

instead of

....

....

I need Your comfort. . .

....

....

....

....

....

I am so thankful for all the ways You love and care for me, including. . .

....

....

....

....

Thank You, Father, for hearing my prayers. *Amen.*

So we have no reason to despair. Despite the fact that our outer humanity is falling apart and decaying, our inner humanity is breathing in new life every day.
2 CORINTHIANS 4:16 VOICE

DATE:

Dear Heavenly Father, ...
....
....
....
....
....

Today I am afraid. . .
....
....
....
....
....
....
....
....
....

(and I'm giving ALL my
fears to You!)

I need Your strength
and courage in these
areas of my life. . .
....
....
....
....
....
....
....
....
....
....
....
....
....
....

I need Your help focusing my thoughts on. . .

....

....

instead of

....

....

I need Your comfort. . . ....

....

....

....

....

I am so thankful for all the ways You
love and care for me, including. . .

....

....

....

....

....

Thank You, Father, for hearing my prayers. *Amen.*

*Here is the bottom line: do not worry about your
life. Don't worry about what you will eat or what
you will drink. Don't worry about how you clothe
your body. Living is about more than merely eating,
and the body is about more than dressing up.*
MATTHEW 6:25 VOICE

DATE:

Dear Heavenly Father, ...
....
....
....
....
....

Today I am afraid. . .
....
....
....
....
....
....
....
....
....
....

(and I'm giving ALL my
fears to You!)

I need Your strength
and courage in these
areas of my life. . .

....
....
....
....
....
....
....
....
....
....
....
....
....
....

I need Your help focusing my thoughts on. . .

....

....

instead of

....

....

I need Your comfort. . .

....

....

....

....

I am so thankful for all the ways You love and care for me, including. . .

....

....

....

....

Thank You, Father, for hearing my prayers. *Amen.*

"Because I, your GOD, have a firm grip on you and I'm not letting go. I'm telling you, 'Don't panic. I'm right here to help you.'"
ISAIAH 41:13 MSG

Dear Heavenly Father, ...
....
....
....
....
....

Today I am afraid. . .

....
....
....
....
....
....
....
....
....
....

(and I'm giving ALL my
fears to You!)

I need Your strength
and courage in these
areas of my life. . .

....
....
....
....
....
....
....
....
....
....
....
....
....
....

I need Your help focusing my thoughts on. . .

....

....

instead of

....

....

I need Your comfort. . .

....

....

....

....

I am so thankful for all the ways You
love and care for me, including. . .

....

....

....

....

Thank You, Father, for hearing my prayers. *Amen.*

Know I am with you, and I will watch over you no matter
where you go. One day I will bring you back to this land.
I will not leave you until I have done all I have promised you.
GENESIS 28:15 VOICE

DATE:

Dear Heavenly Father, ...
....
....
....
....
....

Today I am afraid. . .
....
....
....
....
....
....
....
....
....
....

(and I'm giving ALL my fears to You!)

I need Your strength and courage in these areas of my life. . .
....
....
....
....
....
....
....
....
....
....
....
....
....
....

I need Your help focusing my thoughts on. . .

....

....

instead of

....

....

I need Your comfort. . .

....

....

....

....

I am so thankful for all the ways You
love and care for me, including. . .

....

....

....

....

Thank You, Father, for hearing my prayers. *Amen.*

*"All he has is human strength, but we have the LORD
our God, who will help us fight our battles!"*
2 CHRONICLES 32:8 CEB

DATE:

Dear Heavenly Father,

Today I am afraid. . .

(and I'm giving ALL my fears to You!)

I need Your strength and courage in these areas of my life. . .

I need Your help focusing my thoughts on. . .

....

....

instead of

....

....

I need Your comfort. . . ....

....

....

....

....

I am so thankful for all the ways You love and care for me, including. . .

....

....

....

....

Thank You, Father, for hearing my prayers. *Amen.*

Even in the unending shadows of death's darkness,
I am not overcome by fear. Because You are
with me in those dark moments, near with Your
protection and guidance, I am comforted.
PSALM 23:4 VOICE

Dear Heavenly Father, ...
....
....
....
....
....

Today I am afraid. . .
....
....
....
....
....
....
....
....
....
....

(and I'm giving ALL my
fears to You!)

I need Your strength
and courage in these
areas of my life. . .
....
....
....
....
....
....
....
....
....
....
....
....
....
....

I need Your help focusing my thoughts on. . .

....

....

instead of

....

....

I need Your comfort. . .

....

....

....

....

I am so thankful for all the ways You love and care for me, including. . .

....

....

....

....

Thank You, Father, for hearing my prayers. *Amen.*

So why would I fear the future? Only goodness and tender love pursue me all the days of my life. Then afterward, when my life is through, I'll return to your glorious presence to be forever with you!
PSALM 23:6 TPT

Dear Heavenly Father,

....
....
....
....
....

Today I am afraid. . .

....
....
....
....
....
....
....
....
....
....

(and I'm giving ALL my
fears to You!)

I need Your strength
and courage in these
areas of my life. . .

....
....
....
....
....
....
....
....
....
....
....

I need Your help focusing my thoughts on. . .

....

....

instead of

....

....

I need Your comfort. . .

....

....

....

....

I am so thankful for all the ways You love and care for me, including. . .

....

....

....

....

Thank You, Father, for hearing my prayers. *Amen.*

I cried out to the Lord, "God, come and save me!" He was so kind, so gracious to me. Because of his passion toward me, he made everything right and he restored me.
PSALM 116:4–5 TPT

DATE:

Dear Heavenly Father, ...
....
....
....
....
....

Today I am afraid. . .
....
....
....
....
....
....
....
....
....

(and I'm giving ALL my
fears to You!)

I need Your strength
and courage in these
areas of my life. . .

....
....
....
....
....
....
....
....
....
....
....

I need Your help focusing my thoughts on. . .

....

....

instead of

....

....

I need Your comfort. . .

....

....

....

....

....

I am so thankful for all the ways You love and care for me, including. . .

....

....

....

....

Thank You, Father, for hearing my prayers. *Amen.*

So we can say with great confidence:
"I know the Lord is for me and I will never
be afraid of what people may do to me!"
HEBREWS 13:6 TPT

DATE:

Dear Heavenly Father,

Today I am afraid. . .

(and I'm giving ALL my
fears to You!)

I need Your strength
and courage in these
areas of my life. . .

I need Your help focusing my thoughts on. . .

....

....

instead of

....

....

I need Your comfort. . .

....

....

....

....

I am so thankful for all the ways You
love and care for me, including. . .

....

....

....

....

Thank You, Father, for hearing my prayers. *Amen.*

*"Our tomorrows are in the Lord's hands and if he is
willing we will live life to its fullest and do this or that."*
JAMES 4:15 TPT

DATE:

Dear Heavenly Father,
....
....
....
....
....

Today I am afraid. . .
....
....
....
....
....
....
....
....
....
....
....

(and I'm giving ALL my
fears to You!)

I need Your strength
and courage in these
areas of my life. . .
....
....
....
....
....
....
....
....
....
....
....
....
....
....

I need Your help focusing my thoughts on. . .

....

....

instead of

....

....

I need Your comfort. . .

....

....

....

....

I am so thankful for all the ways You
love and care for me, including. . .

....

....

....

....

Thank You, Father, for hearing my prayers. *Amen.*

*When I had nothing, desperate and defeated,
I cried out to the Lord and he heard me, bringing
his miracle-deliverance when I needed it most.*
PSALM 34:6 TPT

DATE:

Dear Heavenly Father, ...
....
....
....
....
....

Today I am afraid. . .
....
....
....
....
....
....
....
....
....

(and I'm giving ALL my
fears to You!)

I need Your strength
and courage in these
areas of my life. . .
....
....
....
....
....
....
....
....
....
....
....

I need Your help focusing my thoughts on. . .

....

....

instead of

....

....

I need Your comfort. . .

....

....

....

....

I am so thankful for all the ways You
love and care for me, including. . .

....

....

....

....

Thank You, Father, for hearing my prayers. *Amen.*

*You direct me on the path that leads to a beautiful
life. As I walk with You, the pleasures are never-
ending, and I know true joy and contentment.*
PSALM 16:11 VOICE

DATE:

Dear Heavenly Father, ...
....
....
....
....
....

Today I am afraid. . .
....
....
....
....
....
....
....
....

(and I'm giving ALL my
fears to You!)

I need Your strength
and courage in these
areas of my life. . .
....
....
....
....
....
....
....
....
....
....
....
....

I need Your help focusing my thoughts on. . .

....

....

instead of

....

....

I need Your comfort. . .

....

....

....

....

I am so thankful for all the ways You
love and care for me, including. . .

....

....

....

....

Thank You, Father, for hearing my prayers. *Amen.*

*The fear of man brings a snare, but whoever
leans on, trusts in, and puts his confidence
in the Lord is safe and set on high.*
PROVERBS 29:25 AMPC

DATE:

Dear Heavenly Father, ...
....
....
....
....
....

Today I am afraid. . .
....
....
....
....
....
....
....
....
....
....

(and I'm giving ALL my
fears to You!)

I need Your strength
and courage in these
areas of my life. . .
....
....
....
....
....
....
....
....
....
....
....
....
....
....

I need Your help focusing my thoughts on. . .

....

....

instead of

....

....

I need Your comfort. . .

....

....

....

....

I am so thankful for all the ways You
love and care for me, including. . .

....

....

....

....

Thank You, Father, for hearing my prayers. *Amen.*

*Taste of His goodness; see how wonderful the
Eternal truly is. Anyone who puts trust in
Him will be blessed and comforted.*
PSALM 34:8 VOICE

113

Dear Heavenly Father,
....
....
....
....
....
....

Today I am afraid. . .
....
....
....
....
....
....
....
....
....
....
....

(and I'm giving ALL my
fears to You!)

I need Your strength
and courage in these
areas of my life. . .
....
....
....
....
....
....
....
....
....
....
....
....
....
....

I need Your help focusing my thoughts on. . .

instead of

I need Your comfort. . .

I am so thankful for all the ways You
love and care for me, including. . .

Thank You, Father, for hearing my prayers. *Amen.*

*Give us help for the hard task; human help
is worthless. In God we'll do our very best;
he'll flatten the opposition for good.*
PSALM 60:11–12 MSG

115

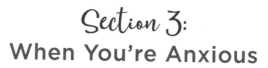

Section 3:
When You're Anxious

ANXIETY CHECK!

Do not be anxious about anything, but in every situation, by prayer and petition, with thanksgiving, present your requests to God.
PHILIPPIANS 4:6 NIV

Today's women are always checking things. A bank balance. E-mail. Text messages. The grocery list. And, of course, that never-ending to-do list. We routinely get our oil, tires, and brake fluid checked. And we wouldn't think of leaving home for the day without checking our appearance in the mirror. We even double-check our purses, making sure we have the essentials—lipstick, mascara, and our cell phone.

Yes, checking is a part of living, isn't it? We do it without even realizing it. Checking to make sure we've locked the door, turned off the stove, and unplugged the flat iron just comes naturally. So why do we forget some of the bigger checks in life? Take anxiety, for instance.

When was the last time you did an anxiety check? Days? Weeks? Months? Chances are you're due for another. After all, we're instructed not to be anxious about anything. Instead, we're to present our requests to God with thanksgiving in our hearts. We're to turn to Him in prayer so that He can take our burdens. Once they've lifted, it's bye-bye anxiety!

Father, I get anxious sometimes. And I don't always remember to turn to You with my anxiety. In fact, I forget to check for anxiety at all. Today I hand my anxieties to You. Thank You that I can present my requests to You.

Date:

Dear Heavenly Father,

Today, I am feeling anxious about...

I confess...

I trust that You will...

My soul needs. . .

_____
_____
_____
_____

I am grateful for. . .

_____
_____
_____
_____
_____

Other things that I need to share with You, God. . .

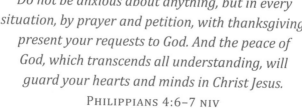

_____
_____
_____
_____

Thank You, Father, for hearing my prayers. *Amen.*

Do not be anxious about anything, but in every situation, by prayer and petition, with thanksgiving, present your requests to God. And the peace of God, which transcends all understanding, will guard your hearts and minds in Christ Jesus.

PHILIPPIANS 4:6–7 NIV

119

Date:

Dear Heavenly Father,

Today, I am feeling anxious about. . .

I confess. . .

I trust that You will. . .

120

My soul needs. . .

I am grateful for. . .

Other things that I need to share with You, God. . .

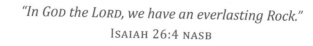

Thank You, Father, for hearing my prayers. *Amen.*

"In God the Lord, we have an everlasting Rock."
Isaiah 26:4 nasb

Date:

Dear Heavenly Father, ...
....
....
....
....

Today, I am feeling anxious about. . .
....
....
....
....
....
....
....
....
....

I confess. . .
....
....
....
....
....
....
....
....
....

I trust that You will. . .
....
....
....
....
....

My soul needs. . .

....
....
....
....

I am grateful for. . .

....
....
....
....
....

Other things that I need to share with
You, God. . .

....
....
....
....
....

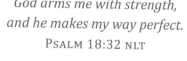
Thank You, Father, for hearing my prayers. *Amen.*

God arms me with strength,
and he makes my way perfect.
PSALM 18:32 NLT

Date:

Dear Heavenly Father, ...
....
....
....
....

Today, I am feeling anxious about. . .
....
....
....
....
....
....
....
....
....

I confess. . .
....
....
....
....
....
....
....
....

I trust that You will. . .
....
....
....
....
....

My soul needs. . .

....

....

....

....

I am grateful for. . .

....

....

....

....

....

Other things that I need to share with
You, God. . .

....

....

....

....

....

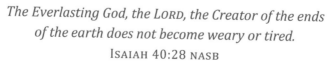

Thank You, Father, for hearing my prayers. *Amen.*

*The Everlasting God, the LORD, the Creator of the ends
of the earth does not become weary or tired.*
ISAIAH 40:28 NASB

Date:

Dear Heavenly Father, ...
....
....
....
....

Today, I am feeling anxious about. . .
....
....
....
....
....
....
....
....
....

I confess. . .
....
....
....
....
....
....
....
....

I trust that You will. . .
....
....
....
....
....

My soul needs. . .

I am grateful for. . .

Other things that I need to share with You, God. . .

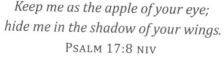
Thank You, Father, for hearing my prayers. _Amen._

Keep me as the apple of your eye;
hide me in the shadow of your wings.
PSALM 17:8 NIV

Date:

Dear Heavenly Father,

Today, I am feeling anxious about. . .

I confess. . .

I trust that You will. . .

My soul needs. . .

....
....
....
....

I am grateful for. . . ....
....
....
....
....
....

Other things that I need to share with You, God. . .

....
....
....
....
....

Thank You, Father, for hearing my prayers. *Amen.*

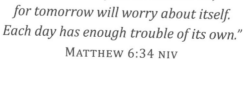

"Do not worry about tomorrow,
for tomorrow will worry about itself.
Each day has enough trouble of its own."
MATTHEW 6:34 NIV

Date:

Dear Heavenly Father, ...
....
....
....
....

Today, I am feeling anxious about. . .
....
....
....
....
....
....
....
....

I confess. . .
....
....
....
....
....
....
....
....

I trust that You will. . .
....
....
....
....
....

My soul needs. . .

I am grateful for. . .

Other things that I need to share with You, God. . .

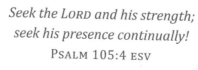

Thank You, Father, for hearing my prayers. _Amen._

Seek the LORD and his strength;
seek his presence continually!
PSALM 105:4 ESV

Date:

Dear Heavenly Father,...
....
....
....
....

Today, I am feeling anxious about. . .
....
....
....
....
....
....
....
....
....

I confess. . .
....
....
....
....
....
....
....
....
....

I trust that You will. . .
....
....
....
....
....

My soul needs. . .

I am grateful for. . .

Other things that I need to share with You, God. . .

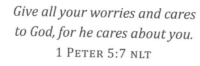

Thank You, Father, for hearing my prayers. *Amen.*

*Give all your worries and cares
to God, for he cares about you.*
1 PETER 5:7 NLT

Date:

Dear Heavenly Father, ...
....
....
....
....

Today, I am feeling anxious about. . .
....
....
....
....
....
....
....
....
....

I confess. . .
....
....
....
....
....
....
....
....
....

I trust that You will. . .
....
....
....
....

My soul needs. . .

I am grateful for. . .

Other things that I need to share with You, God. . .

Thank You, Father, for hearing my prayers. *Amen.*

Rest in the LORD, and wait patiently for him.
PSALM 37:7 KJV

135

Date:

Dear Heavenly Father,...
....
....
....
....

Today, I am feeling anxious about. . .
....
....
....
....
....
....
....
....

I confess. . .
....
....
....
....
....
....
....

I trust that You will. . .
....
....
....
....
....

My soul needs. . .

I am grateful for. . .

Other things that I need to share with You, God. . .

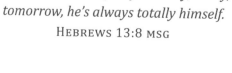

Thank You, Father, for hearing my prayers. _Amen._

Jesus doesn't change—yesterday, today,
tomorrow, he's always totally himself.
HEBREWS 13:8 MSG

Date:

Dear Heavenly Father, ...
....
....
....
....

Today, I am feeling anxious about. . .
....
....
....
....
....
....
....
....
....

I confess. . .
....
....
....
....
....
....
....
....
....

I trust that You will. . .
....
....
....
....
....

My soul needs. . .

....
....
....
....

I am grateful for. . .

....
....
....
....
....
....

Other things that I need to share with You, God. . .

....
....
....
....
....

Thank You, Father, for hearing my prayers. *Amen.*

*Let us therefore come boldly unto the
throne of grace, that we may obtain mercy,
and find grace to help in time of need.*
HEBREWS 4:16 KJV

Date: ....

Dear Heavenly Father, ...
....
....
....
....

Today, I am feeling anxious about. . .
....
....
....
....
....
....
....
....

I confess. . .
....
....
....
....
....
....
....

I trust that You will. . .
....
....
....
....
....

My soul needs. . .

I am grateful for. . .

Other things that I need to share with You, God. . .

Thank You, Father, for hearing my prayers. _Amen._

"I will trust, and will not be afraid; for the LORD GOD is my strength and my song, and he has become my salvation."
ISAIAH 12:2 ESV

Date:

Dear Heavenly Father,...
....
....
....
....

Today, I am feeling anxious about. . .
....
....
....
....
....
....
....
....
....

I confess. . .
....
....
....
....
....
....
....
....
....

I trust that You will. . .
....
....
....
....
....

My soul needs. . .

_____
_____
_____
_____

I am grateful for. . .

_____
_____
_____
_____
_____

Other things that I need to share with You, God. . .

_____
_____
_____
_____

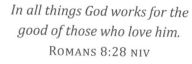
Thank You, Father, for hearing my prayers. *Amen.*

In all things God works for the
good of those who love him.
ROMANS 8:28 NIV

Date:

Dear Heavenly Father,...
....
....
....
....

Today, I am feeling anxious about. . .
....
....
....
....
....
....
....
....

I confess. . .
....
....
....
....
....
....
....
....

I trust that You will. . .
....
....
....
....
....

My soul needs. . .

I am grateful for. . .

Other things that I need to share with You, God. . .

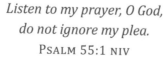

Thank You, Father, for hearing my prayers. _Amen._

Listen to my prayer, O God,
do not ignore my plea.
PSALM 55:1 NIV

145

Date:

Dear Heavenly Father,

Today, I am feeling anxious about. . .

I confess. . .

I trust that You will. . .

My soul needs. . .

I am grateful for. . .

Other things that I need to share with You, God. . .

Thank You, Father, for hearing my prayers. *Amen.*

Now faith is the assurance of things hoped for,
the conviction of things not seen.
HEBREWS 11:1 ESV

Date: ....

Dear Heavenly Father, ...
....
....
....
....

Today, I am feeling anxious about. . .
....
....
....
....
....
....
....
....
....

I confess. . .
....
....
....
....
....
....
....
....

I trust that You will. . .
....
....
....
....

My soul needs. . .

_____
_____
_____
_____

I am grateful for. . .

_____
_____
_____
_____
_____

Other things that I need to share with
You, God. . .

_____
_____
_____
_____
_____

Thank You, Father, for hearing my prayers. *Amen.*

*In my distress I called to the LORD. . . . He heard my
voice; my cry came before him, into his ears.*
PSALM 18:6 NIV

149

Date:

Dear Heavenly Father, ...
....
....
....
....

Today, I am feeling anxious about. . .
....
....
....
....
....
....
....
....
....

I confess. . .
....
....
....
....
....
....
....
....

I trust that You will. . .
....
....
....
....

My soul needs. . .

I am grateful for. . .

Other things that I need to share with You, God. . .

Thank You, Father, for hearing my prayers. *Amen.*

As soon as I pray, you answer me;
you encourage me by giving me strength.
PSALM 138:3 NLT

Date:

Dear Heavenly Father, ...
....
....
....
....

Today, I am feeling anxious about. . .
....
....
....
....
....
....
....
....

I confess. . .
....
....
....
....
....
....
....
....
....

I trust that You will. . .
....
....
....
....
....

My soul needs. . .

I am grateful for. . .

Other things that I need to share with
You, God. . .

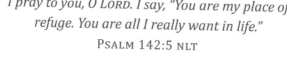
Thank You, Father, for hearing my prayers. _Amen._

_I pray to you, O LORD. I say, "You are my place of
refuge. You are all I really want in life."_
PSALM 142:5 NLT

Date:

Dear Heavenly Father, ...
....
....
....
....

Today, I am feeling anxious about. . .
....
....
....
....
....
....
....
....
....
....

I confess. . .
....
....
....
....
....
....
....
....

I trust that You will. . .
....
....
....
....
....

My soul needs. . .

I am grateful for. . .

Other things that I need to share with You, God. . .

Thank You, Father, for hearing my prayers. _Amen._

The LORD is good to those who wait for him, to the soul who seeks him.
LAMENTATIONS 3:25 ESV

Date:

Dear Heavenly Father,

Today, I am feeling anxious about. . .

I confess. . .

I trust that You will. . .

My soul needs. . .

I am grateful for. . .

Other things that I need to share with You, God. . .

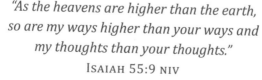

Thank You, Father, for hearing my prayers. _Amen._

"As the heavens are higher than the earth,
so are my ways higher than your ways and
my thoughts than your thoughts."
ISAIAH 55:9 NIV

Date:

Dear Heavenly Father,

Today, I am feeling anxious about. . .

I confess. . .

I trust that You will. . .

My soul needs. . .

I am grateful for. . .

Other things that I need to share with You, God. . .

Thank You, Father, for hearing my prayers. *Amen.*

But I'm in the very presence of God—
oh, how refreshing it is!
PSALM 73:28 MSG

159

Date:

Dear Heavenly Father, ...
....
....
....
....

Today, I am feeling anxious about. . .
....
....
....
....
....
....
....
....

I confess. . .
....
....
....
....
....
....
....
....

I trust that You will. . .
....
....
....
....

My soul needs. . .

....

....

....

....

I am grateful for. . .

....

....

....

....

Other things that I need to share with
You, God. . .

....

....

....

....

Thank You, Father, for hearing my prayers. *Amen.*

*Search me, God, and know my heart; put me to the test
and know my anxious thoughts; and see if there is any
hurtful way in me, and lead me in the everlasting way.*
PSALM 139:23–24 NASB

Date:

Dear Heavenly Father,

Today, I am feeling anxious about. . .

I confess. . .

I trust that You will. . .

My soul needs. . .

_____
_____
_____
_____

I am grateful for. . .

_____
_____
_____
_____

Other things that I need to share with You, God. . .

_____
_____
_____
_____

Thank You, Father, for hearing my prayers. *Amen.*

I am counting on the LORD;
yes, I am counting on him.
PSALM 130:5 NLT

Date:

Dear Heavenly Father, ...
....
....
....
....

Today, I am feeling anxious about. . .
....
....
....
....
....
....
....
....
....

I confess. . .
....
....
....
....
....
....
....
....

I trust that You will. . .
....
....
....
....
....

My soul needs. . .

....
....
....
....

I am grateful for. . .

....
....
....
....
....

Other things that I need to share with You, God. . .

....
....
....
....
....

Thank You, Father, for hearing my prayers. *Amen.*

*"No one who trusts God like this—
heart and soul—will ever regret it."*
ROMANS 10:11 MSG

Date:

Dear Heavenly Father, ...
....
....
....
....

Today, I am feeling anxious about. . .
....
....
....
....
....
....
....
....
....
....

I confess. . .
....
....
....
....
....
....
....
....
....

I trust that You will. . .
....
....
....
....
....

My soul needs. . .

I am grateful for. . .

Other things that I need to share with You, God. . .

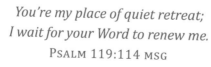

Thank You, Father, for hearing my prayers. _Amen._

You're my place of quiet retreat;
I wait for your Word to renew me.
PSALM 119:114 MSG

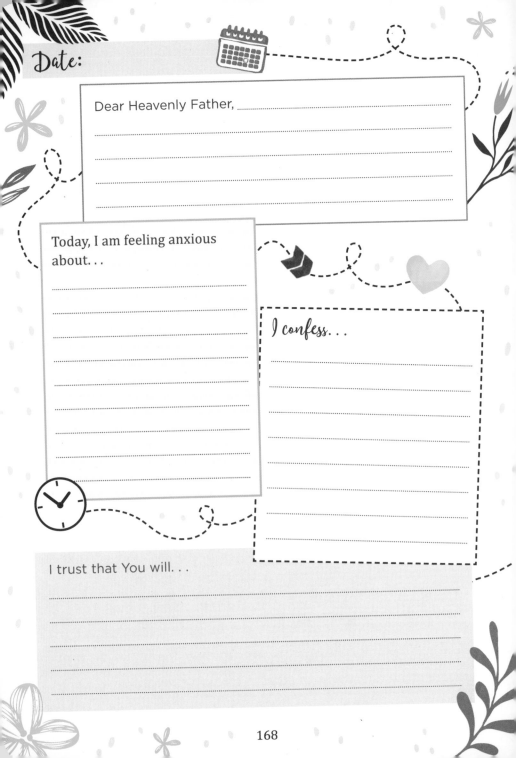

Date:

Dear Heavenly Father,

Today, I am feeling anxious about. . .

I confess. . .

I trust that You will. . .

My soul needs. . .

....
....
....
....

I am grateful for. . .

....
....
....
....
....
....

Other things that I need to share with
You, God. . .

....
....
....
....
....

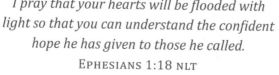

Thank You, Father, for hearing my prayers. *Amen.*

*I pray that your hearts will be flooded with
light so that you can understand the confident
hope he has given to those he called.*
Ephesians 1:18 NLT

Section 4:
When You're Going through a Difficult Time

LAY IT AT THE CROSS

"Come to me, all you who are weary and burdened, and I will give you rest. Take my yoke upon you and learn from me. . .you will find rest for your souls. For my yoke is easy and my burden is light."
MATTHEW 11:28–30 NIV

Does life sometimes get you down? Often when we experience difficulties that weigh us down, we hear the old adage "Lay it at the cross." But how do we lay our difficulties at the cross?

Jesus gives us step-by-step guidance in how to place our difficulties and burdens at the foot of the cross. First, He invites us to come to Him; those of us who are weary and burdened just need to approach Jesus in prayer. Second, He exchanges our heavy and burdensome load with His easy and light load. Jesus gives us His yoke and encourages us to learn from Him. The word *yoke* refers to Christ's teachings, Jesus' *way* of living life. As we follow His teachings, we take His yoke in humility and gentleness, surrendering and submitting ourselves to His will and ways for our lives. Finally, we praise God for the rest He promises to provide us.

Do you have any difficulties in life, any burdens, worries, fears, relationship issues, finance troubles, or work problems that you need to "lay at the cross"? Jesus says, "Come."

Lord, thank You for inviting me to come and exchange my heavy burden for Your light burden. I praise You for the rest You promise me. Amen.

Date:

Dear Heavenly Father, ...
....
....
....
....
....

Today my heart is troubled because. . .
....
....
....
....
....
....
....
....
....

(but with You by my side,
I am comforted!)

I'm feeling. . .
....
....
....
....
....
....
....
....
....
....
....
....
....

I need Your comfort. . .

....
....
....
....
....
....
....
....
....
....
....
....
....
....
....
....
....
....
....

Even when life is difficult,
You provide many blessings,
including. . .

....
....
....
....
....
....
....
....
....
....

Thank You, Father, for hearing my prayers. *Amen.*

As for God, his way is perfect: The LORD's word is
flawless; he shields all who take refuge in him.
PSALM 18:30 NIV

173

Date:

Dear Heavenly Father, ...
....
....
....
....
....

Today my heart is troubled because. . .
....
....
....
....
....
....
....
....
....

(but with You by my side,
I am comforted!)

I'm feeling. . .
....
....
....
....
....
....
....
....
....
....
....
....

I need Your comfort. . .

Even when life is difficult,
You provide many blessings,
including. . .

Thank You, Father, for hearing my prayers. *Amen.*

He tends his flock like a shepherd:
He gathers the lambs in his arms and
carries them close to his heart.
ISAIAH 40:11 NIV

Date:

Dear Heavenly Father, ...
....
....
....
....
....

Today my heart is troubled because. . .
....
....
....
....
....
....
....
....
....
....

(but with You by my side,
I am comforted!)

I'm feeling. . .
....
....
....
....
....
....
....
....
....
....
....
....
....

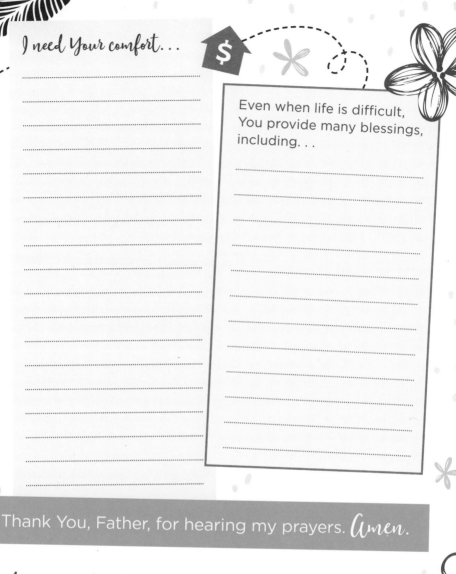

I need Your comfort. . .

....
....
....
....
....
....
....
....
....
....
....
....
....
....
....
....
....
....
....

Even when life is difficult, You provide many blessings, including. . .

....
....
....
....
....
....
....
....
....
....
....

Thank You, Father, for hearing my prayers. *Amen.*

Many are the afflictions of the righteous, but the LORD delivers him out of them all.
PSALM 34:19 ESV

Date:

Dear Heavenly Father, ...
....
....
....
....
....

Today my heart is troubled because. . .
....
....
....
....
....
....
....
....
....

(but with You by my side,
I am comforted!)

I'm feeling. . .
....
....
....
....
....
....
....
....
....
....
....
....
....

I need Your comfort. . .

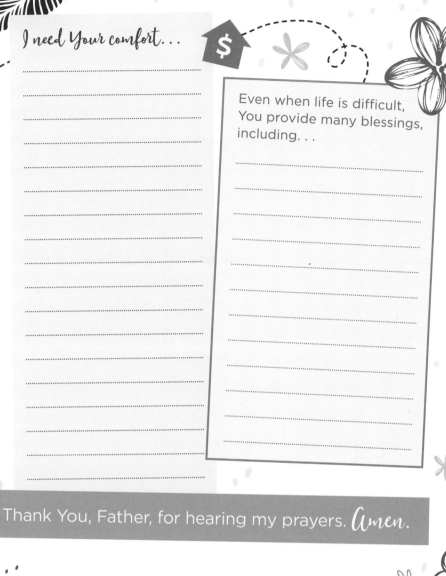

....
....
....
....
....
....
....
....
....
....
....
....
....
....
....
....

Even when life is difficult,
You provide many blessings,
including. . .

....
....
....
....
....
....
....
....
....
....

Thank You, Father, for hearing my prayers. *Amen*.

"You, LORD, are my lamp; the LORD
turns my darkness into light."
2 SAMUEL 22:29 NIV

Date:

Dear Heavenly Father, ...
....
....
....
....
....

Today my heart is troubled because. . .
....
....
....
....
....
....
....
....
....

(but with You by my side,
I am comforted!)

I'm feeling. . .
....
....
....
....
....
....
....
....
....
....
....
....

I need Your comfort...

Even when life is difficult,
You provide many blessings,
including. . .

Thank You, Father, for hearing my prayers. *Amen.*

"Let not your heart be troubled."
JOHN 14:1 NKJV

Date:

Dear Heavenly Father, ...
....
....
....
....
....

Today my heart is troubled because. . .
....
....
....
....
....
....
....
....
....
....
....

(but with You by my side,
I am comforted!)

I'm feeling. . .
....
....
....
....
....
....
....
....
....
....
....
....
....
....

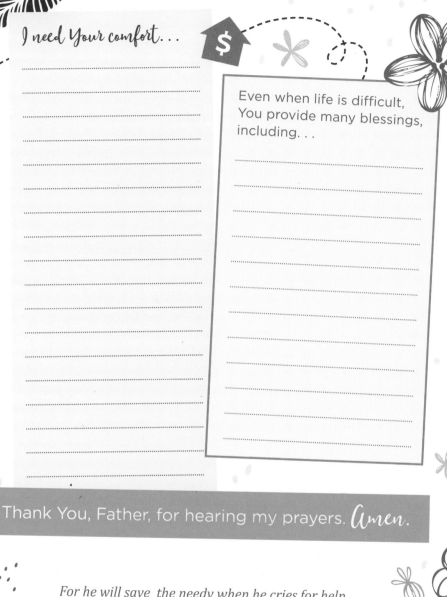

I need Your comfort...

Even when life is difficult,
You provide many blessings,
including. . .

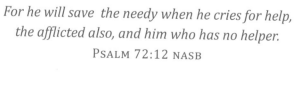

Thank You, Father, for hearing my prayers. *Amen.*

*For he will save the needy when he cries for help,
the afflicted also, and him who has no helper.*
Psalm 72:12 NASB

Date:

Dear Heavenly Father, ...
....
....
....
....
....

Today my heart is troubled because. . .
....
....
....
....
....
....
....
....
....
....

(but with You by my side,
I am comforted!)

I'm feeling. . .
....
....
....
....
....
....
....
....
....
....
....
....
....

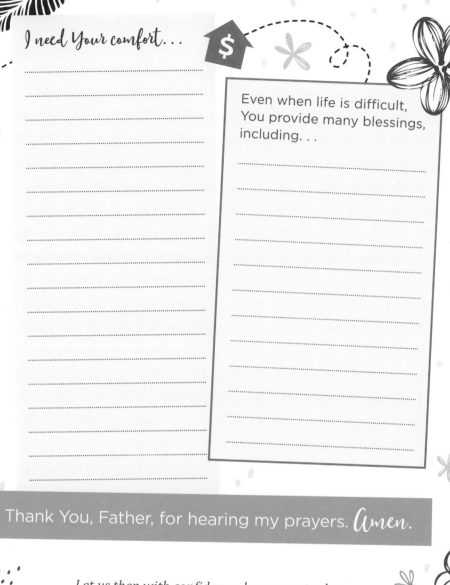

I need Your comfort...

Even when life is difficult,
You provide many blessings,
including. . .

Thank You, Father, for hearing my prayers. *Amen.*

*Let us then with confidence draw near to the
throne of grace, that we may receive mercy
and find grace to help in time of need.*
HEBREWS 4:16 ESV

Date:

Dear Heavenly Father, ...
....
....
....
....
....

Today my heart is troubled because. . .
....
....
....
....
....
....
....
....
....

(but with You by my side,
I am comforted!)

I'm feeling. . .
....
....
....
....
....
....
....
....
....
....
....
....

I need Your comfort...

....
....
....
....
....
....
....
....
....
....
....
....
....
....
....

Even when life is difficult,
You provide many blessings,
including. . .

....
....
....
....
....
....
....
....
....

Thank You, Father, for hearing my prayers. *Amen.*

The Lord's unfailing love surrounds
the one who trusts in him.
PSALM 32:10 NIV

Date:

Dear Heavenly Father, ...
....
....
....
....
....

Today my heart is troubled because. . .
....
....
....
....
....
....
....
....
....
....

(but with You by my side,
I am comforted!)

I'm feeling. . .
....
....
....
....
....
....
....
....
....
....
....
....
....
....

I need Your comfort. . .

....
....
....
....
....
....
....
....
....
....
....
....
....
....
....
....
....

Even when life is difficult,
You provide many blessings,
including. . .

....
....
....
....
....
....
....
....
....
....
....

Thank You, Father, for hearing my prayers. *Amen.*

*"I have told you these things, so that in me you may
have peace. In this world you will have trouble.
But take heart! I have overcome the world."*
JOHN 16:33 NIV

Date:

Dear Heavenly Father,

Today my heart is troubled because...

(but with You by my side,
I am comforted!)

I'm feeling...

190

I need Your comfort...

....
....
....
....
....
....
....
....
....
....
....
....
....
....
....
....
....
....
....

Even when life is difficult,
You provide many blessings,
including. . .

....
....
....
....
....
....
....
....
....
....

Thank You, Father, for hearing my prayers. *Amen.*

*May the God of hope fill you with all joy and
peace in believing, so that by the power of
the Holy Spirit you may abound in hope.*
ROMANS 15:13 ESV

Dear Heavenly Father, ...
....
....
....
....
....

Today my heart is troubled because. . .
....
....
....
....
....
....
....
....
....
....
....

(but with You by my side,
I am comforted!)

I'm feeling. . .
....
....
....
....
....
....
....
....
....
....
....
....
....

I need Your comfort...

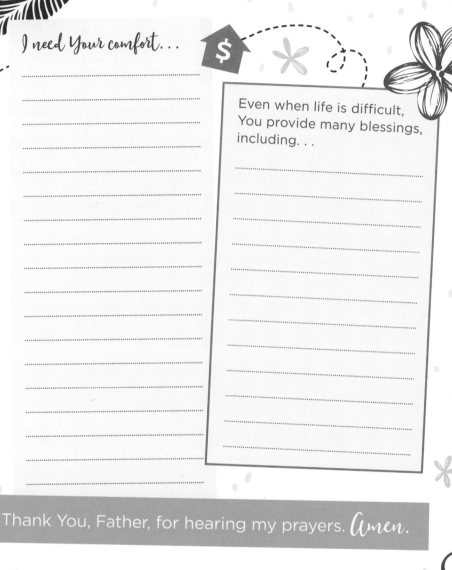

....
....
....
....
....
....
....
....
....
....
....
....
....
....
....
....
....

Even when life is difficult,
You provide many blessings,
including. . .

....
....
....
....
....
....
....
....
....
....
....

Thank You, Father, for hearing my prayers. *Amen.*

*"For truly, I say to you, if you have faith like
a grain of mustard seed, you will say to this
mountain, 'Move from here to there,' and it will
move, and nothing will be impossible for you."*
Matthew 17:20 esv

Date: _____

Dear Heavenly Father, ...
....
....
....
....
....
....

Today my heart is troubled because. . .
....
....
....
....
....
....
....
....
....

(but with You by my side,
I am comforted!)

I'm feeling. . .
....
....
....
....
....
....
....
....
....
....
....
....
....
....

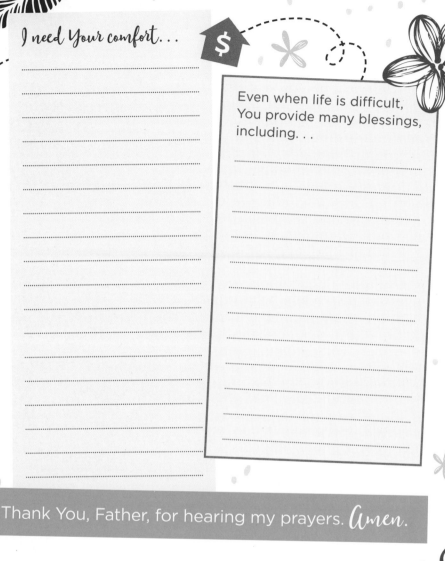

I need Your comfort...

....
....
....
....
....
....
....
....
....
....
....
....
....
....
....
....
....
....
....

Even when life is difficult, You provide many blessings, including. . .

....
....
....
....
....
....
....
....
....
....
....
....
....
....

Thank You, Father, for hearing my prayers. *Amen.*

"Call to me and I will answer you, and will tell you great and hidden things that you have not known."
JEREMIAH 33:3 ESV

Date:

Dear Heavenly Father, ...
....
....
....
....
....

Today my heart is troubled because. . .
....
....
....
....
....
....
....
....
....

(but with You by my side,
I am comforted!)

I'm feeling. . .
....
....
....
....
....
....
....
....
....
....
....
....

I need Your comfort. . .

Even when life is difficult,
You provide many blessings,
including. . .

Thank You, Father, for hearing my prayers. *Amen.*

The LORD is a refuge for the oppressed,
a stronghold in times of trouble.
PSALM 9:9 NIV

Date:

Dear Heavenly Father, ...
....
....
....
....
....

Today my heart is troubled because. . .
....
....
....
....
....
....
....
....
....
....

(but with You by my side,
I am comforted!)

I'm feeling. . .
....
....
....
....
....
....
....
....
....
....
....
....
....

I need Your comfort. . .

....
....
....
....
....
....
....
....
....
....
....
....
....
....
....
....

Even when life is difficult,
You provide many blessings,
including. . .

....
....
....
....
....
....
....
....
....
....

Thank You, Father, for hearing my prayers. *Amen.*

God has said, "I will never leave you;
I will never abandon you."
HEBREWS 13:5 NCV

Date:

Dear Heavenly Father, ...
....
....
....
....
....

Today my heart is troubled because. . .
....
....
....
....
....
....
....
....
....

(but with You by my side,
I am comforted!)

I'm feeling. . .
....
....
....
....
....
....
....
....
....
....
....
....

I need Your comfort. . .

....
....
....
....
....
....
....
....
....
....
....
....
....
....
....
....
....
....

Even when life is difficult,
You provide many blessings,
including. . .

....
....
....
....
....
....
....
....
....
....
....

Thank You, Father, for hearing my prayers. *Amen.*

The LORD makes firm the steps of the one who delights in him; though he may stumble, he will not fall, for the LORD upholds him with his hand.
PSALM 37:23–24 NIV

201

Date:

Dear Heavenly Father, ...
....
....
....
....
....

Today my heart is troubled because. . .
....
....
....
....
....
....
....
....
....

(but with You by my side,
I am comforted!)

I'm feeling. . .
....
....
....
....
....
....
....
....
....
....

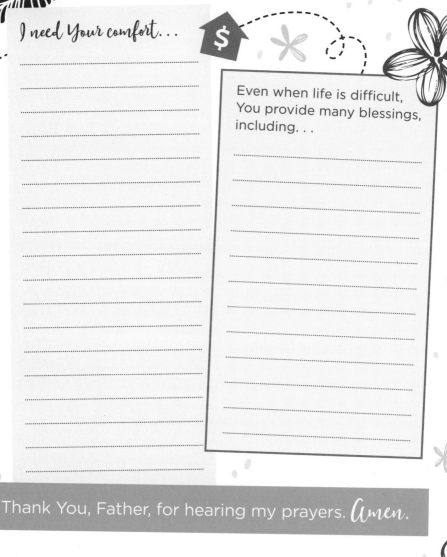

I need Your comfort...

> Even when life is difficult, You provide many blessings, including. . .

Thank You, Father, for hearing my prayers. *Amen.*

But you, LORD, are a shield around me,
my glory, the One who lifts my head high.
PSALM 3:3 NIV

Date:

Dear Heavenly Father,

Today my heart is troubled because. . .

(but with You by my side,
I am comforted!)

I'm feeling. . .

I need Your comfort...

....

....

....

....

....

....

....

....

....

....

....

....

....

....

....

Even when life is difficult, You provide many blessings, including. . .

....

....

....

....

....

....

....

....

....

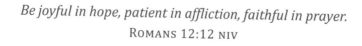

Thank You, Father, for hearing my prayers. *Amen.*

Be joyful in hope, patient in affliction, faithful in prayer.
ROMANS 12:12 NIV

Date:

Dear Heavenly Father,

Today my heart is troubled because. . .

(but with You by my side,
I am comforted!)

I'm feeling. . .

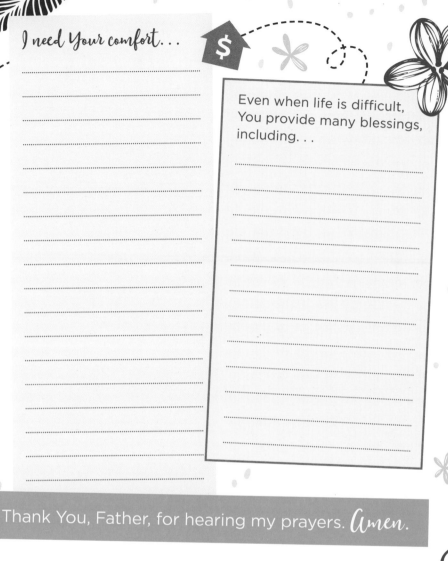

I need Your comfort...

....
....
....
....
....
....
....
....
....
....
....
....
....
....
....
....
....

Even when life is difficult,
You provide many blessings,
including. . .

....
....
....
....
....
....
....
....
....
....

Thank You, Father, for hearing my prayers. *Amen.*

He got up, rebuked the wind and said to the waves,
"Quiet! Be still!" Then the wind died down
and it was completely calm.

MARK 4:39 NIV

Date:

Dear Heavenly Father, ...
....
....
....
....
....

Today my heart is troubled because. . .
....
....
....
....
....
....
....
....
....
....

(but with You by my side,
I am comforted!)

I'm feeling. . .
....
....
....
....
....
....
....
....
....
....
....
....
....

I need Your comfort...

....
....
....
....
....
....
....
....
....
....
....
....
....
....
....
....

Even when life is difficult,
You provide many blessings,
including. . .

....
....
....
....
....
....
....
....
....
....
....

Thank You, Father, for hearing my prayers. *Amen.*

*I called on your name, LORD, from the
depths of the pit. You heard my plea:
"Do not close your ears to my cry for relief."*
LAMENTATIONS 3:55–56 NIV

Date:

Dear Heavenly Father, ...
....
....
....
....
....

Today my heart is troubled because. . .
....
....

I'm feeling. . .

....

(but with You by my side,
I am comforted!)

I need Your comfort. . .

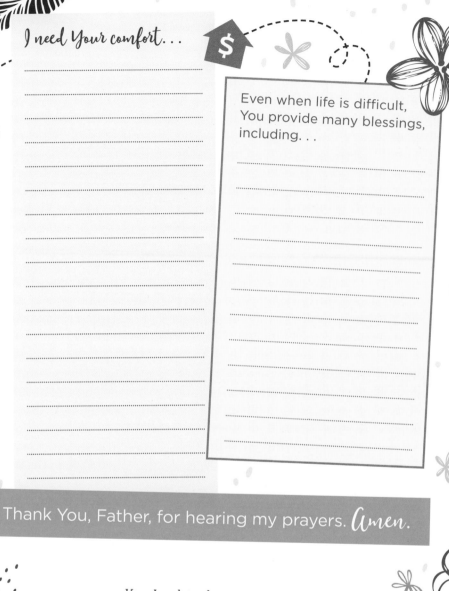

Even when life is difficult,
You provide many blessings,
including. . .

Thank You, Father, for hearing my prayers. *Amen.*

You, Lord, took up my case;
you redeemed my life.
LAMENTATIONS 3:58 NIV

Date:

Dear Heavenly Father, ...
....
....
....
....
....

Today my heart is troubled because. . .
....
....
....
....
....
....
....
....
....
....

(but with You by my side,
I am comforted!)

I'm feeling. . .
....
....
....
....
....
....
....
....
....
....
....
....
....

I need Your comfort. . .

Even when life is difficult, You provide many blessings, including. . .

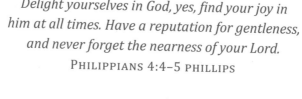

Thank You, Father, for hearing my prayers. *Amen.*

Delight yourselves in God, yes, find your joy in him at all times. Have a reputation for gentleness, and never forget the nearness of your Lord.
PHILIPPIANS 4:4–5 PHILLIPS

Date:

Dear Heavenly Father, ...
....
....
....
....
....

Today my heart is troubled because. . .
....
....
....
....
....
....
....
....
....
....

(but with You by my side,
I am comforted!)

I'm feeling. . .
....
....
....
....
....
....
....
....
....
....
....
....

I need Your comfort...

....

....

....

....

....

....

....

....

....

....

....

....

....

....

Even when life is difficult,
You provide many blessings,
including. . .

....

....

....

....

....

....

....

....

Thank You, Father, for hearing my prayers. *Amen.*

We can be full of joy here and now even in our trials and troubles. Taken in the right spirit these very things will give us patient endurance; this in turn will develop a mature character, and a character of this sort produces a steady hope, a hope that will never disappoint us.

ROMANS 5:3–5 PHILLIPS

Date:

Dear Heavenly Father, ...
....
....
....
....
....

Today my heart is troubled because. . .
....
....
....
....
....
....
....
....
....
....
....

(but with You by my side,
I am comforted!)

I'm feeling. . .
....
....
....
....
....
....
....
....
....
....
....
....
....
....

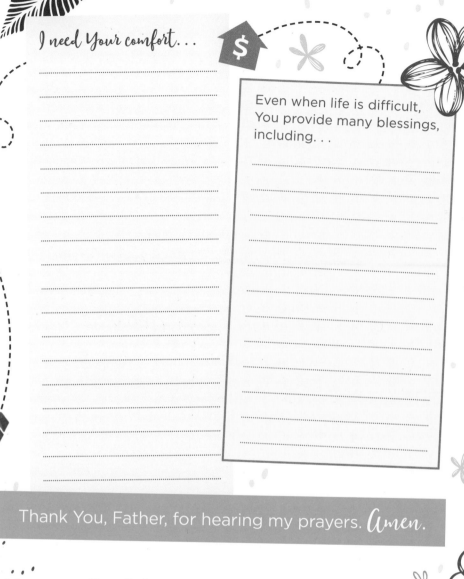

I need Your comfort. . .

Even when life is difficult,
You provide many blessings,
including. . .

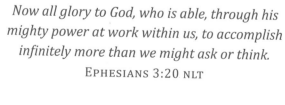

*Now all glory to God, who is able, through his
mighty power at work within us, to accomplish
infinitely more than we might ask or think.*
EPHESIANS 3:20 NLT

Date:

Dear Heavenly Father, ...
....
....
....
....
....

Today my heart is troubled because. . .
....
....
....

I'm feeling. . .

(but with You by my side,
I am comforted!)

I need Your comfort. . .

....
....
....
....
....
....
....
....
....
....
....
....
....
....
....
....
....
....

Even when life is difficult,
You provide many blessings,
including. . .

....
....
....
....
....
....
....
....
....
....
....

Thank You, Father, for hearing my prayers. *Amen.*

*Behold, I stand at the door and knock; if anyone
hears and listens to and heeds My voice and
opens the door, I will come in to him.*
REVELATION 3:20 AMPC

Date:

Dear Heavenly Father, ...
....
....
....
....
....

Today my heart is troubled because. . .
....
....
....
....

I'm feeling. . .

....
....
....
....
....
....

(but with You by my side,
I am comforted!)

I need Your comfort...

....
....
....
....
....
....
....
....
....
....
....
....
....
....
....
....
....
....
....

Even when life is difficult, You provide many blessings, including. . .

....
....
....
....
....
....
....
....
....
....
....

Thank You, Father, for hearing my prayers. *Amen.*

I know that the LORD is great,
that our Lord is greater than all gods.
PSALM 135:5 NIV

Section 5:
When You're Grieving

TEARS

Jesus wept.
JOHN 11:35 NIV

- -

Jesus wept. He cried when He heard the news of the death of His good friend Lazarus. Jesus knew He would bring Lazarus back to life, yet His heart still broke with sadness. Jesus experienced sorrow Himself, and He knows the depth of our pain when we lose someone or something important to us.

Grief is an intense emotion. Knowing that Jesus cried helps us to accept our own weeping—especially when our loss is still fresh.

Sometimes we're embarrassed that our tears stream from a seemingly bottomless well. Yet tears are so precious to God that He records and stores each one. The psalm writer said, "You keep track of all my sorrows. You have collected all my tears in your bottle. You have recorded each one in your book" (Psalm 56:8 NLT).

Jesus' tears demonstrate God's empathy as we go through the grieving process. God cares deeply about our situation. He desires to gather us in His arms. He understands the sorrow and turmoil we feel when we experience serious heartache.

Crying is a natural response to deep pain and loss. Our tears form wordless prayers connecting us with God. He knows the depth of our sorrow. He comforts us with His love and His tears.

> *Loving Lord, You know my tears. You value each of my tears so much that You gather them in Your bottle and write them in Your book. Thank You for understanding me.*

Date:

Dear Heavenly Father, ...
....
....
....
....

Today, I am really missing. . .
....
....
....
....
....
....
....
....
....
....

I feel. . .
....
....
....
....
....
....
....

I need. . .
....
....
....
....

I am grateful for people and things that bring me comfort, like. . .

I am thankful for memories, like. . .

Other things that I need to share with You, God. . .

Thank You, Father, for hearing my prayers and comforting my heart. *Amen.*

"Blessed are those who mourn,
for they will be comforted."
MATTHEW 5:4 NIV

Date: ....

Dear Heavenly Father, ...
....
....
....
....
....

Today, I am really missing. . .
....
....
....
....
....
....
....
....
....
....
....

I feel. . .
....
....
....
....
....
....
....
....

I need. . .
....
....
....
....

I am grateful for people and things that bring me comfort, like. . .

....

....

....

....

I am thankful for memories, like. . .

....

....

....

....

....

Other things that I need to share with You, God. . .

....

....

....

....

Thank You, Father, for hearing my prayers and comforting my heart. *Amen.*

For Christ also suffered once for sins, the righteous for the unrighteous, that he might bring us to God, being put to death in the flesh but made alive in the spirit.
1 PETER 3:18 ESV

Date:

Dear Heavenly Father, ...
....
....
....
....

Today, I am really missing. . .
....
....
....
....
....
....
....
....
....
....

I feel. . .
....
....
....
....
....
....
....
....
....

I need. . .
....
....
....
....

I am grateful for people and things that bring me comfort, like. . .

....

....

....

....

I am thankful for memories, like. . .

....

....

....

....

....

Other things that I need to share with You, God. . .

....

....

....

....

Thank You, Father, for hearing my prayers and comforting my heart. *Amen.*

Be gracious to me, LORD, for I am frail.
PSALM 6:2 NASB

Date:

Dear Heavenly Father, ...
....
....
....
....

Today, I am really missing. . .
....
....
....
....
....
....
....
....
....
....
....

I feel. . .
....
....
....
....
....
....
....
....
....

I need. . .
....
....
....
....

I am grateful for people and things that bring me comfort, like. . .

....

....

....

....

I am thankful for memories, like. . .

....

....

....

....

....

Other things that I need to share with You, God. . .

....

....

....

....

Thank You, Father, for hearing my prayers
and comforting my heart. *Amen.*

*"I will not leave you as orphans;
I will come to you."*
JOHN 14:18 NIV

Date:

Dear Heavenly Father, ...
....
....
....
....

Today, I am really missing. . .
....
....
....
....
....
....
....
....
....
....

I feel. . .
....
....
....
....
....
....
....
....
....

I need. . .
....
....
....
....

I am grateful for people and things that bring me comfort, like. . .

I am thankful for memories, like. . .

Other things that I need to share with You, God. . .

Thank You, Father, for hearing my prayers and comforting my heart. *Amen.*

"'He will wipe every tear from their eyes. There will be no more death' or mourning or crying or pain, for the old order of things has passed away."

REVELATION 21:4 NIV

Date:

Dear Heavenly Father, ...
....
....
....
....

Today, I am really missing. . .
....
....
....
....
....
....
....
....
....
....

I feel. . .
....
....
....
....
....
....
....
....
....

I need. . .
....
....
....
....

I am grateful for people and things that bring me comfort, like. . .

....
....
....
....

I am thankful for memories, like. . .

....
....
....
....
....

Other things that I need to share
with You, God. . .

....
....
....
....

Thank You, Father, for hearing my prayers
and comforting my heart. *Amen.*

*Precious in the sight of the LORD is
the death of his faithful servants.*
PSALM 116:15 NIV

Date:

Dear Heavenly Father, ...
....
....
....
....

Today, I am really missing. . .
....
....
....
....
....
....
....
....
....
....
....

I feel...
....
....
....
....
....
....
....
....

I need...
....
....
....
....

I am grateful for people and things that bring me comfort, like. . .

_____

_____

_____

_____

I am thankful for memories, like. . .

_____

_____

_____

_____

_____

Other things that I need to share
with You, God. . .

_____

_____

_____

_____

Thank You, Father, for hearing my prayers
and comforting my heart. *Amen.*

*Forgetting what is behind and straining toward what
is ahead, I press on toward the goal to win the prize for
which God has called me heavenward in Christ Jesus.*
PHILIPPIANS 3:13–14 NIV

Date:

Dear Heavenly Father, ...
....
....
....
....
....

Today, I am really missing. . .
....
....
....
....
....
....
....
....
....
....

I feel. . .
....
....
....
....
....
....
....
....

I need. . .
....
....
....
....

I am grateful for people and things that bring me comfort, like. . .

....

....

....

....

I am thankful for memories, like. . .

....

....

....

....

....

Other things that I need to share
with You, God. . .

....

....

....

....

Thank You, Father, for hearing my prayers
and comforting my heart. *Amen.*

*"Even to your old age and gray hairs I am he, I am
he who will sustain you. I have made you and I will
carry you; I will sustain you and I will rescue you."*
ISAIAH 46:4 NIV

Date:

Dear Heavenly Father, ...
....
....
....
....

Today, I am really missing. . .
....
....
....
....
....
....
....
....
....
....
....

I feel. . .
....
....
....
....
....
....
....
....
....

I need. . .
....
....
....
....

I am grateful for people and things that bring me comfort, like. . .

_____
_____
_____
_____

I am thankful for memories, like. . .

_____
_____
_____
_____
_____

Other things that I need to share
with You, God. . .

_____
_____
_____
_____

Thank You, Father, for hearing my prayers
and comforting my heart. *Amen.*

*Being confident of this very thing, that He
who has begun a good work in you will
complete it until the day of Jesus Christ.*
PHILIPPIANS 1:6 NKJV

Date:

Dear Heavenly Father, ...
....
....
....
....

Today, I am really missing. . .
....
....
....
....
....
....
....
....
....
....

I feel. . .
....
....
....
....
....
....
....
....

I need. . .
....
....
....
....

I am grateful for people and things that bring me comfort, like. . .

I am thankful for memories, like. . .

Other things that I need to share with You, God. . .

Thank You, Father, for hearing my prayers and comforting my heart. _Amen._

He heals the brokenhearted
and binds up their wounds.
PSALM 147:3 NIV

Date:

Dear Heavenly Father, ...
....
....
....
....

Today, I am really missing. . .
....
....
....
....
....
....
....
....
....
....

I feel. . .
....
....
....
....
....
....
....

I need. . .
....
....
....
....

I am grateful for people and things that bring me comfort, like. . .

I am thankful for memories, like. . .

Other things that I need to share with You, God. . .

Thank You, Father, for hearing my prayers and comforting my heart. *Amen.*

To every thing there is a season, and a time to every purpose under the heaven: a time to be born, and a time to die. . .a time to weep, and a time to laugh; a time to mourn, and a time to dance.
Ecclesiastes 3:1–2, 4 kjv

Date:

Dear Heavenly Father, ...
....
....
....
....

Today, I am really missing. . .
....
....
....
....
....
....
....
....
....
....

I feel. . .
....
....
....
....
....
....
....
....
....

I need. . .
....
....
....
....

I am grateful for people and things that bring me comfort, like. . .

....
....
....
....

I am thankful for memories, like. . .

....
....
....
....
....
....

Other things that I need to share
with You, God. . .

....
....
....
....
....

Thank You, Father, for hearing my prayers
and comforting my heart. *Amen.*

*"My Father's house has many rooms; if that
were not so, would I have told you that I am
going there to prepare a place for you?"*
JOHN 14:2 NIV

Date:

Dear Heavenly Father, ...
....
....
....
....

Today, I am really missing. . .
....
....
....
....
....
....
....
....
....

I feel. . .
....
....
....
....
....
....
....
....

I need. . .
....
....
....
....

I am grateful for people and things that bring me comfort, like. . .

....

....

....

....

I am thankful for memories, like. . .

....

....

....

....

....

Other things that I need to share
with You, God. . .

....

....

....

....

Thank You, Father, for hearing my prayers
and comforting my heart. *Amen.*

*Brothers and sisters, we do not want you to be uninformed
about those who sleep in death, so that you do not
grieve like the rest of mankind, who have no hope.*

1 THESSALONIANS 4:13 NIV

Date:

Dear Heavenly Father, ...
....
....
....
....

Today, I am really missing. . .
....
....
....
....
....
....
....
....
....
....

I feel. . .
....
....
....
....
....
....
....
....
....
....

I need. . .
....
....
....
....

I am grateful for people and things that bring me comfort, like. . .

....

....

....

....

I am thankful for memories, like. . .

....

....

....

....

....

Other things that I need to share
with You, God. . .

....

....

....

....

Thank You, Father, for hearing my prayers
and comforting my heart. *Amen.*

Yet this I call to mind and therefore I have hope:
Because of the LORD's great love we are not
consumed, for his compassions never fail. They are
new every morning; great is your faithfulness.
LAMENTATIONS 3:21–23 NIV

Date:

Dear Heavenly Father, ...
....
....
....
....

Today, I am really missing. . .
....
....
....
....
....
....
....
....
....
....

I feel. . .
....
....
....
....
....
....
....
....

I need. . .
....
....
....
....

I am grateful for people and things that bring me comfort, like. . .

....

....

....

....

I am thankful for memories, like. . .

....

....

....

....

....

Other things that I need to share
with You, God. . .

....

....

....

....

Thank You, Father, for hearing my prayers
and comforting my heart. *Amen.*

*Surely goodness and mercy shall follow
me all the days of my life, and I shall
dwell in the house of the Lord forever.*
PSALM 23:6 ESV

Date:

Dear Heavenly Father, ...
....
....
....
....

Today, I am really missing. . .
....
....
....
....
....
....
....
....
....
....

I feel. . .
....
....
....
....
....
....
....
....
....
....

I need. . .
....
....
....
....

I am grateful for people and things that bring me comfort, like. . .

I am thankful for memories, like. . .

Other things that I need to share with You, God. . .

Thank You, Father, for hearing my prayers and comforting my heart. *Amen.*

"Be still, and know that I am God."
PSALM 46:10 ESV

Date:

Dear Heavenly Father, ...
....
....
....
....

Today, I am really missing. . .
....
....
....
....
....
....
....
....
....
....

I feel. . .
....
....
....
....
....
....
....
....

I need. . .
....
....
....

I am grateful for people and things that bring me comfort, like. . .

_____
_____
_____
_____

I am thankful for memories, like. . .

_____
_____
_____
_____
_____

Other things that I need to share
with You, God. . .

_____
_____
_____
_____

Thank You, Father, for hearing my prayers
and comforting my heart. *Amen.*

*For I consider that the sufferings of this
present time are not worth comparing
with the glory that is to be revealed to us.*
ROMANS 8:18 ESV

Date:

Dear Heavenly Father, ...
....
....
....
....

Today, I am really missing. . .
....
....
....
....
....
....
....
....
....
....

I feel. . .
....
....
....
....
....
....
....
....

I need. . .
....
....
....
....

I am grateful for people and things that bring me comfort, like. . .

....

....

....

....

I am thankful for memories, like. . .

....

....

....

....

....

Other things that I need to share
with You, God. . .

....

....

....

....

Thank You, Father, for hearing my prayers
and comforting my heart. *Amen.*

Be merciful to me, LORD, for I am in distress;
my eyes grow weak with sorrow,
my soul and body with grief.
PSALM 31:9 NIV

Date:

Dear Heavenly Father, ...
....
....
....
....

Today, I am really missing. . .
....
....
....
....
....
....
....
....
....

I feel. . .
....
....
....
....
....
....
....
....

I need. . .
....
....
....
....

I am grateful for people and things that bring me comfort, like. . .

I am thankful for memories, like. . .

Other things that I need to share with You, God. . .

Thank You, Father, for hearing my prayers and comforting my heart. _Amen._

So we fix our eyes not on what is seen,
but on what is unseen, since what is seen
is temporary, but what is unseen is eternal.
2 CORINTHIANS 4:18 NIV

Date:

Dear Heavenly Father, ...
....
....
....
....

Today, I am really missing. . .
....
....
....
....
....
....
....
....
....
....

I feel. . .
....
....
....
....
....
....
....
....
....
....

I need. . .
....
....
....
....

I am grateful for people and things that bring me comfort, like. . .

....

....

....

....

I am thankful for memories, like. . .

....

....

....

....

Other things that I need to share
with You, God. . .

....

....

....

....

Thank You, Father, for hearing my prayers
and comforting my heart. *Amen.*

My comfort in my suffering is this:
Your promise preserves my life.
PSALM 119:50 NIV

Date: ....

Dear Heavenly Father, ...
....
....
....
....

Today, I am really missing. . .
....
....
....
....
....
....
....
....
....

I feel. . .
....
....
....
....
....
....
....
....
....

I need. . .
....
....
....
....

I am grateful for people and things that bring me comfort, like. . .

....
....
....
....

I am thankful for memories, like. . .

....
....
....
....
....

Other things that I need to share
with You, God. . .

....
....
....
....
....

Thank You, Father, for hearing my prayers
and comforting my heart. *Amen.*

Listen, I tell you a mystery: We will not
all sleep, but we will all be changed.
1 CORINTHIANS 15:51 NIV

Date:

Dear Heavenly Father, ...
....
....
....
....

Today, I am really missing. . .
....
....
....
....
....
....
....
....
....
....

I feel. . .
....
....
....
....
....
....
....
....

I need. . .
....
....
....
....

I am grateful for people and things that bring me comfort, like. . .

....

....

....

....

I am thankful for memories, like. . .

....

....

....

....

....

Other things that I need to share
with You, God. . .

....

....

....

....

Thank You, Father, for hearing my prayers
and comforting my heart. *Amen.*

*You make known to me the path of life;
you will fill me with joy in your presence,
with eternal pleasures at your right hand.*
PSALM 16:11 NIV

Date:

Dear Heavenly Father, ...
....
....
....
....

Today, I am really missing. . .
....
....
....
....
....
....
....
....
....
....

I feel. . .
....
....
....
....
....
....
....
....
....

I need. . .
....
....
....
....

I am grateful for people and things that bring me comfort, like. . .

I am thankful for memories, like. . .

Other things that I need to share with You, God. . .

Thank You, Father, for hearing my prayers and comforting my heart. Amen.

But do not overlook this one fact, beloved, that with the Lord one day is as a thousand years, and a thousand years as one day.
2 PETER 3:8 ESV

Date:

Dear Heavenly Father, ...
....
....
....
....

Today, I am really missing. . .
....
....
....
....
....
....
....
....
....
....
....

I feel. . .
....
....
....
....
....
....
....
....

I need. . .
....
....
....
....

I am grateful for people and things that bring me comfort, like. . .

....

....

....

....

I am thankful for memories, like. . .

....

....

....

....

....

Other things that I need to share
with You, God. . .

....

....

....

....

Thank You, Father, for hearing my prayers
and comforting my heart. *Amen.*

*Jesus said. . . , "I am the resurrection
and the life. The one who believes in
me will live, even though they die."*
JOHN 11:25 NIV

Date:

Dear Heavenly Father, ...
....
....
....
....

Today, I am really missing. . .
....
....
....
....
....
....
....
....
....
....

I feel. . .
....
....
....
....
....
....
....
....
....

I need. . .
....
....
....
....

I am grateful for people and things that bring me comfort, like. . .

I am thankful for memories, like. . .

Other things that I need to share with You, God. . .

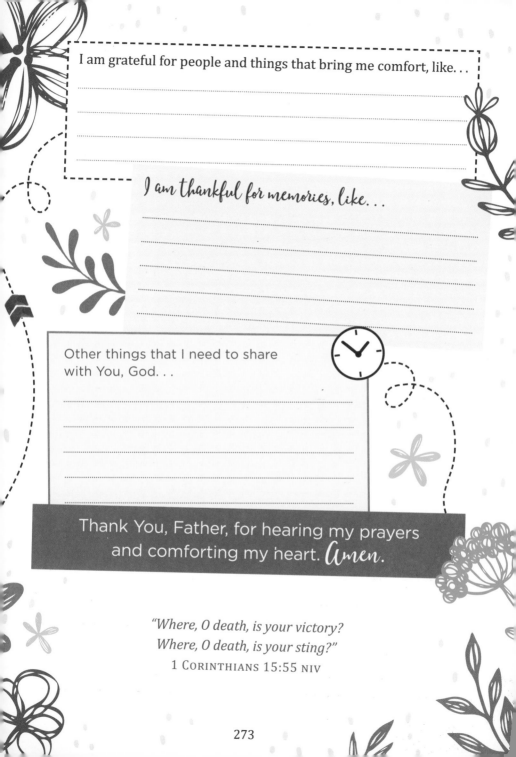

Thank You, Father, for hearing my prayers and comforting my heart. _Amen._

"Where, O death, is your victory?
Where, O death, is your sting?"
1 CORINTHIANS 15:55 NIV

Date: _____

Dear Heavenly Father, ...
....
....
....
....

Today, I am really missing. . .
....
....
....
....
....
....
....
....
....

I feel. . .
....
....
....
....
....
....
....
....

I need. . .
....
....
....

274

I am grateful for people and things that bring me comfort, like. . .

....

....

....

....

I am thankful for memories, like. . .

....

....

....

....

Other things that I need to share
with You, God. . .

....

....

....

Thank You, Father, for hearing my prayers
and comforting my heart. Amen.

*"For God so loved the world, that He gave His
only Son, so that everyone who believes in
Him will not perish, but have eternal life."*
JOHN 3:16 NASB

Section 6:
When You Need Hope and Healing

AMNON AND TAMAR

And Tamar lived in her brother Absalom's house, a desolate woman.
2 SAMUEL 13:20 NIV

Second Samuel 13 tells the tragic story of Amnon and Tamar. Amnon, one of King David's sons, raped his half sister, Tamar. Verse 18 says that Tamar dressed appropriately as a virgin daughter of the king. But after she was raped, Tamar exchanged her beautiful robe for the ashes of mourning.

Absalom, Tamar's other brother, was kind to her and took her into his home. Although she lived with him, scripture says that Absalom never said a word about her pain. The last time we read of Tamar is in 2 Samuel 13:20, "And Tamar lived in her brother Absalom's house, a desolate woman." Unfortunately, because of the culture of the time, Tamar would no longer be considered marriageable. The stigma of rape would remain with her, and this one event would shape the rest of Tamar's life.

Many women today also have been victimized. After experiencing pain and victimization, they, like Tamar, live desolate lives, allowing the experience to define them and determine their future. This does not have to be. Unlike Tamar, women today have choices.

No matter how dark your circumstances, God can redeem them. He can weave your pain into the tapestry of your life and provide hope, help, and healing. You can begin by speaking of the pain, then refusing to carry it. Open your heart to God today and receive the gift of healing.

> *Father, thank You for offering me hope and healing.*
> *Help me to let go of the pain of my past so that it does*
> *not define me. Redeem it for Your glory. Amen.*

Date:

Dear Heavenly Father, ...
....
....
....
....
....

Today, I am feeling troubled about. . .
....
....
....
....
....
....
....

I need Your hope. . .
....
....
....
....
....
....
....
....

Please bring healing to. . .
....
....
....
....

My soul needs Your comforting touch in these areas. . .

I am thankful for. . .

Other things that I need to share with You, God. . .

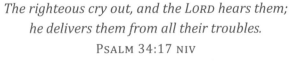

Thank You, Father, for hearing my prayers. _Amen._

The righteous cry out, and the LORD hears them;
he delivers them from all their troubles.
PSALM 34:17 NIV

Date:

Dear Heavenly Father, ...
....
....
....
....
....

Today, I am feeling troubled about. . .
....
....
....
....
....
....
....
....
....

I need Your hope. . .
....
....
....
....
....
....
....
....

Please bring healing to. . .
....
....
....
....
....

My soul needs Your comforting touch in these areas. . .

I am thankful for. . .

Other things that I need to share
with You, God. . .

Thank You, Father, for hearing my prayers. *Amen.*

May integrity and uprightness protect me,
because my hope, LORD, is in you.
PSALM 25:21 NIV

Date:

Dear Heavenly Father, ...
....
....
....
....
....

Today, I am feeling troubled about. . .
....
....
....
....
....
....
....

I need Your hope. . .
....
....
....
....
....
....
....
....
....

Please bring healing to. . .
....
....
....
....
....

My soul needs Your comforting touch in these areas. . .

....
....
....
....

I am thankful for. . .

....
....
....
....
....
....

Other things that I need to share
with You, God. . .

....
....
....
....
....

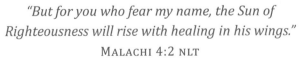

Thank You, Father, for hearing my prayers. *Amen.*

*"But for you who fear my name, the Sun of
Righteousness will rise with healing in his wings."*
MALACHI 4:2 NLT

Date:

Dear Heavenly Father, ...
....
....
....
....
....

Today, I am feeling troubled about. . .
....
....
....
....
....
....
....
....

I need Your hope. . .
....
....
....
....
....
....
....
....

Please bring healing to. . .
....
....
....
....
....

My soul needs Your comforting touch in these areas. . .

I am thankful for. . .

Other things that I need to share
with You, God. . .

Thank You, Father, for hearing my prayers. _Amen._

_Fear the LORD and turn away from evil. Then you will
have healing for your body and strength for your bones._
PROVERBS 3:7–8 NLT

Date:

Dear Heavenly Father,

Today, I am feeling troubled about. . .

I need Your hope. . .

Please bring healing to. . .

My soul needs Your comforting touch in these areas. . .

I am thankful for. . .

Other things that I need to share
with You, God. . .

Thank You, Father, for hearing my prayers. *Amen.*

*May the God of hope fill you with all joy and
peace in believing, so that by the power of
the Holy Spirit you may abound in hope.*
ROMANS 15:13 ESV

Date:

Dear Heavenly Father, ...
....
....
....
....
....

Today, I am feeling troubled about. . .
....
....
....
....
....
....
....

I need Your hope. . .
....
....
....
....
....
....
....
....

Please bring healing to. . .
....
....
....
....
....

My soul needs Your comforting touch in these areas. . .

I am thankful for. . .

Other things that I need to share with You, God. . .

Thank You, Father, for hearing my prayers. _Amen._

Seek the LORD and his strength;
seek his presence continually!
PSALM 105:4 ESV

Date:

Dear Heavenly Father, ...
....
....
....
....
....

Today, I am feeling troubled about. . .
....
....
....
....
....
....
....
....

I need Your hope. . .
....
....
....
....
....
....
....
....
....

Please bring healing to. . .
....
....
....
....
....

My soul needs Your comforting touch in these areas. . .

I am thankful for. . .

Other things that I need to share
with You, God. . .

Thank You, Father, for hearing my prayers. *Amen.*

But you, LORD, are a shield around me,
my glory, the One who lifts my head high.
PSALM 3:3 NIV

Date:

Dear Heavenly Father, ...
....
....
....
....
....

Today, I am feeling troubled about. . .

....
....
....
....
....
....
....
....

I need Your hope. . .

....
....
....
....
....
....
....
....
....
....

Please bring healing to. . .

....
....
....
....
....

My soul needs Your comforting touch in these areas. . .

I am thankful for. . .

Other things that I need to share
with You, God. . .

Thank You, Father, for hearing my prayers. _Amen._

Now, may the Lord himself, the Lord of
peace, pour into you his peace in every
circumstance and in every possible way.
The Lord's tangible presence be with you all.
2 Thessalonians 3:16 tpt

Date:

Dear Heavenly Father, ...
....
....
....
....
....

Today, I am feeling troubled about. . .
....
....
....
....
....
....
....
....

I need Your hope. . .
....
....
....
....
....
....
....
....

Please bring healing to. . .
....
....
....
....

My soul needs Your comforting touch in these areas. . .

I am thankful for. . .

Other things that I need to share with You, God. . .

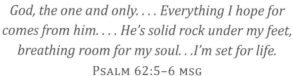

Thank You, Father, for hearing my prayers. *Amen.*

*God, the one and only. . . . Everything I hope for
comes from him. . . . He's solid rock under my feet,
breathing room for my soul. . .I'm set for life.*
PSALM 62:5–6 MSG

Date:

Dear Heavenly Father,..
....
....
....
....

Today, I am feeling troubled about. . .
....
....
....
....
....
....
....

I need Your hope. . .
....
....
....
....
....
....
....
....

Please bring healing to. . .
....
....
....
....
....

My soul needs Your comforting touch in these areas. . .

I am thankful for. . .

Other things that I need to share
with You, God. . .

Thank You, Father, for hearing my prayers. _Amen._

_Pray about everything. He longs to hear your
requests, so talk to God about your needs
and be thankful for what has come._
PHILIPPIANS 4:6 VOICE

Date:

Dear Heavenly Father, ...
....
....
....
....
....

Today, I am feeling troubled about. . .
....
....
....
....
....
....

I need Your hope. . .
....
....
....
....
....
....
....

Please bring healing to. . .
....
....
....
....
....

My soul needs Your comforting touch in these areas. . .

I am thankful for. . .

Other things that I need to share with You, God. . .

Thank You, Father, for hearing my prayers. *Amen.*

Those who walk the fields to sow, casting their
seed in tears, will one day tread those same
long rows, amazed by what's appeared.
PSALM 126:5 VOICE

Date:

Dear Heavenly Father,

Today, I am feeling troubled about. . .

I need Your hope. . .

Please bring healing to. . .

My soul needs Your comforting touch in these areas. . .

I am thankful for. . .

Other things that I need to share
with You, God. . .

Thank You, Father, for hearing my prayers. *Amen.*

*If your faith remains strong, even while
surrounded by life's difficulties, you will continue
to experience the untold blessings of God!*
JAMES 1:12 TPT

Date:

Dear Heavenly Father, ...
....
....
....
....
....

Today, I am feeling troubled about. . .
....
....
....
....
....
....
....
....

I need Your hope. . .
....
....
....
....
....
....
....
....
....

Please bring healing to. . .
....
....
....
....
....

My soul needs Your comforting touch in these areas. . .

I am thankful for. . .

Other things that I need to share with You, God. . .

Thank You, Father, for hearing my prayers. *Amen.*

Give God the right to direct your life,
and as you trust him along the way
you'll find he pulled it off perfectly!
PSALM 37:5 TPT

Date:

Dear Heavenly Father, ...
....
....
....
....
....

Today, I am feeling troubled about. . .
....
....
....
....
....
....
....
....

I need Your hope. . .
....
....
....
....
....
....
....
....
....
....

Please bring healing to. . .
....
....
....
....
....

My soul needs Your comforting touch in these areas. . .

I am thankful for. . .

Other things that I need to share
with You, God. . .

Thank You, Father, for hearing my prayers. _Amen._

_So now you need to rethink everything and turn to God
so your sins will be forgiven and a new day can dawn,
days of refreshing times flowing from the Lord._
ACTS 3:19 VOICE

Date:

Dear Heavenly Father, ...
....
....
....
....
....

Today, I am feeling troubled about. . .
....
....
....
....
....
....
....
....

I need Your hope. . .
....
....
....
....
....
....
....
....
....

Please bring healing to. . .
....
....
....
....
....

My soul needs Your comforting touch in these areas. . .

I am thankful for. . .

Other things that I need to share
with You, God. . .

Thank You, Father, for hearing my prayers. *Amen.*

*So I say to my soul, "Don't be discouraged. Don't be disturbed.
For I know my God will break through for me." Then I'll
have plenty of reasons to praise him all over again.*

PSALM 42:11 TPT

Date:

Dear Heavenly Father, ...
....
....
....
....
....

Today, I am feeling troubled about. . .
....
....
....
....
....
....
....

I need Your hope. . .
....
....
....
....
....
....
....

Please bring healing to. . .
....
....
....
....
....

My soul needs Your comforting touch in these areas. . .

I am thankful for. . .

Other things that I need to share with You, God. . .

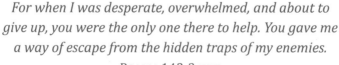

Thank You, Father, for hearing my prayers. *Amen.*

For when I was desperate, overwhelmed, and about to give up, you were the only one there to help. You gave me a way of escape from the hidden traps of my enemies.
PSALM 142:3 TPT

Date:

Dear Heavenly Father,

Today, I am feeling troubled about. . .

I need Your hope. . .

Please bring healing to. . .

My soul needs Your comforting touch in these areas. . .

_____
_____
_____
_____

I am thankful for. . .

_____
_____
_____
_____
_____

Other things that I need to share
with You, God. . .

_____
_____
_____
_____
_____

Thank You, Father, for hearing my prayers. *Amen.*

Let your unfailing love surround us, LORD,
for our hope is in you alone.
PSALM 33:22 NLT

311

Date:

Dear Heavenly Father,

Today, I am feeling troubled about. . .

I need Your hope. . .

Please bring healing to. . .

My soul needs Your comforting touch in these areas. . .

I am thankful for. . .

Other things that I need to share
with You, God. . .

Thank You, Father, for hearing my prayers. *Amen.*

And [Jesus] said. . . , "Daughter, your faith has made
you well; go in peace and be cured of your disease."
MARK 5:34 NASB

Date:

Dear Heavenly Father, ...
....
....
....
....
....

Today, I am feeling troubled about. . .
....
....
....
....
....
....
....

I need Your hope. . .
....
....
....
....
....
....
....

Please bring healing to. . .
....
....
....
....
....

My soul needs Your comforting touch in these areas. . .

I am thankful for. . .

Other things that I need to share
with You, God. . .

Thank You, Father, for hearing my prayers. _Amen._

_Guide me in your truth and teach me, for you are God
my Savior, and my hope is in you all day long._
PSALM 25:5 NIV

Date:

Dear Heavenly Father,

Today, I am feeling troubled about. . .

I need Your hope. . .

Please bring healing to. . .

My soul needs Your comforting touch in these areas. . .

I am thankful for. . .

Other things that I need to share with You, God. . .

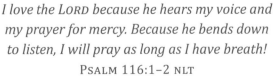

Thank You, Father, for hearing my prayers. *Amen.*

I love the LORD because he hears my voice and my prayer for mercy. Because he bends down to listen, I will pray as long as I have breath!
PSALM 116:1–2 NLT

Date:

Dear Heavenly Father, ...
....
....
....
....
....

Today, I am feeling troubled about. . .
....
....
....
....
....
....
....
....

I need Your hope. . .
....
....
....
....
....
....
....
....
....

Please bring healing to. . .
....
....
....
....
....

My soul needs Your comforting touch in these areas. . .

I am thankful for. . .

Other things that I need to share
with You, God. . .

Thank You, Father, for hearing my prayers. _Amen._

Desperate, I throw myself on you: you are my God! Hour by
hour I place my days in your hand. . . . What a stack of blessing
you have piled up for those who worship you, ready and
waiting for all who run to you to escape an unkind world.
PSALM 31:14–15, 19 MSG

Date:

Dear Heavenly Father, ...
....
....
....
....
....

Today, I am feeling troubled about. . .
....
....
....
....
....
....
....

I need Your hope. . .
....
....
....
....
....
....
....
....

Please bring healing to. . .
....
....
....
....
....

My soul needs Your comforting touch in these areas. . .

I am thankful for. . .

Other things that I need to share
with You, God. . .

Thank You, Father, for hearing my prayers. _Amen._

Hear this. . .stand still and consider
the wondrous works of God.
JOB 37:14 AMPC

Date:

Dear Heavenly Father, ...
....
....
....
....
....

Today, I am feeling troubled about. . .
....
....
....
....
....
....
....
....
....

I need Your hope. . .
....
....
....
....
....
....
....
....
....
....

Please bring healing to. . .
....
....
....
....

My soul needs Your comforting touch in these areas. . .

I am thankful for. . .

Other things that I need to share with You, God. . .

Thank You, Father, for hearing my prayers. *Amen.*

Likewise the Spirit helps us in our weakness. For we do not know what to pray for as we ought, but the Spirit himself intercedes for us with groanings too deep for words.
ROMANS 8:26 ESV

Date:

Dear Heavenly Father, ...

....

....

....

....

....

Today, I am feeling troubled about. . .

....

....

....

....

....

....

I need Your hope. . .

....

....

....

....

....

....

....

Please bring healing to. . .

....

....

....

....

My soul needs Your comforting touch in these areas. . .

I am thankful for. . .

Other things that I need to share with You, God. . .

Thank You, Father, for hearing my prayers. *Amen.*

If you don't know what you're doing, pray to the Father. He loves to help. You'll get his help, and won't be condescended to when you ask for it. Ask boldly, believingly, without a second thought.
JAMES 1:5–6 MSG

Date:

Dear Heavenly Father, ...
....
....
....
....
....

Today, I am feeling troubled about. . .
....
....
....
....
....
....
....
....

I need Your hope. . .
....
....
....
....
....
....
....
....
....

Please bring healing to. . .
....
....
....
....
....

My soul needs Your comforting touch in these areas. . .

I am thankful for. . .

Other things that I need to share
with You, God. . .

Thank You, Father, for hearing my prayers. *Amen*.

The hopes of the godly result in happiness.
PROVERBS 10:28 NLT

Section 7:
When You're Stressed Out

HIS PERFECT STRENGTH

"My grace is sufficient for you, for my power is made perfect in weakness." Therefore I will boast all the more gladly about my weaknesses, so that Christ's power may rest on me.
2 Corinthians 12:9 NIV

How do you define stress? Perhaps you feel it when the car doesn't start or the toilet backs up or the line is too long at the grocery store. Or maybe your source of stress is a terrible diagnosis, a late-night phone call, a demanding boss, or a broken relationship. It's probably a combination of all of these things. You might be able to cope with one of them, but when several are bearing down at once, stress is the inevitable result.

It has been said that stress results when our perceived demands exceed our perceived resources. When the hours required to meet a deadline at work (demand) exceed the number of hours we have available (resources), we get stressed. The most important word in this definition is *perceived*. When it comes to stress, people have a tendency to do two things. One, they magnify the demand ("I will *never* be able to get this done") and two, they fail to consider all of their resources. For the child of God, this includes His mighty strength, which remains long after ours is gone.

In an uncertain world, it is difficult to say few things for sure. But no matter what life throws our way, we can be confident of this: our demands will *never* exceed God's vast resources.

> *Strong and mighty heavenly Father, thank You that in my weakness I can always rely on Your perfect strength. Amen.*

DATE:

Dear Heavenly Father, _____
_____
_____
_____
_____
_____

Today I am stressed because. . .
_____
_____
_____
_____
_____
_____
_____
_____
_____
_____
_____

(and I'm giving it all to You!)

I'm feeling. . .
_____
_____
_____
_____
_____
_____
_____
_____
_____
_____
_____
_____
_____
_____
_____

I need Your help focusing my thoughts on. . .

....

....

instead of

....

....

I need Your guidance with. . .

....

....

....

....

Help me to be thankful for all of life's blessings (big and small!), including. . .

....

....

....

....

Thank You, Father, for hearing my prayers. *Amen.*

*"Give in to God, come to terms with him and
everything will turn out just fine. Let him tell
you what to do; take his words to heart."*
JOB 22:21–22 MSG

DATE:

Dear Heavenly Father, ...
....
....
....
....
....

Today I am stressed because. . .
....
....
....
....
....
....
....
....
....
....

(and I'm giving it all to You!)

I'm feeling. . .
....
....
....
....
....
....
....
....
....
....
....
....
....
....
....

I need Your help focusing my thoughts on. . .

....

....

instead of

....

....

I need Your guidance with. . ...

....

....

....

....

Help me to be thankful for all of life's blessings (big and small!), including. . .

....

....

....

....

Thank You, Father, for hearing my prayers. *Amen.*

Trust GOD from the bottom of your heart; don't try to figure out everything on your own. Listen for GOD's voice in everything you do, everywhere you go; he's the one who will keep you on track.
PROVERBS 3:5–6 MSG

DATE:

Dear Heavenly Father,

Today I am stressed because. . .

(and I'm giving it all to You!)

I'm feeling. . .

I need Your help focusing my thoughts on. . .

....

....

instead of

....

....

I need Your guidance with. . . ..

....

....

....

....

Help me to be thankful for all of life's blessings (big and small!), including. . .

....

....

....

....

Thank You, Father, for hearing my prayers. *Amen.*

*I'm not trying to win the approval of people,
but of God. If pleasing people were my goal,
I would not be Christ's servant.*
GALATIANS 1:10 NLT

DATE:

Dear Heavenly Father,

Today I am stressed because. . .

(and I'm giving it all to You!)

I'm feeling. . .

I need Your help focusing my thoughts on. . .

....

....

instead of

....

....

I need Your guidance with. . . ..

....

....

....

....

Help me to be thankful for all of life's
blessings (big and small!), including. . .

....

....

....

....

Thank You, Father, for hearing my prayers. *Amen.*

[It is] the Spirit of God that made me [which has
stirred me up], and the breath of the Almighty
that gives me life [which inspires me].
JOB 33:4 AMPC

DATE:

Dear Heavenly Father,

Today I am stressed because. . .

(and I'm giving it all to You!)

I'm feeling. . .

338

I need Your help focusing my thoughts on. . .

....

....

instead of

....

....

I need Your guidance with. . . ..

....

....

....

....

Help me to be thankful for all of life's blessings (big and small!), including. . .

....

....

....

....

Thank You, Father, for hearing my prayers. *Amen.*

"Oh, how my soul praises the Lord.
How my spirit rejoices in God my Savior!"
LUKE 1:46–47 NLT

DATE:

Dear Heavenly Father, ...
....
....
....
....
....

Today I am stressed because. . .
....
....
....
....
....
....
....
....
....
....
....

(and I'm giving it all to You!)

I'm feeling. . .
....
....
....
....
....
....
....
....
....
....
....
....
....
....

340

I need Your help focusing my thoughts on. . .

....

....

instead of

....

....

I need Your guidance with. . . ..

....

....

....

....

Help me to be thankful for all of life's blessings (big and small!), including. . .

....

....

....

....

Thank You, Father, for hearing my prayers. *Amen.*

The minute I said, "I'm slipping, I'm falling," your love, GOD, took hold and held me fast. When I was upset and beside myself, you calmed me down and cheered me up.
PSALM 94:18–19 MSG

DATE:

Dear Heavenly Father,

Today I am stressed because. . .

(and I'm giving it all to You!)

I'm feeling. . .

342

I need Your help focusing my thoughts on. . .

....

....

instead of

....

....

I need Your guidance with. . .

....

....

....

....

Help me to be thankful for all of life's
blessings (big and small!), including. . .

....

....

....

....

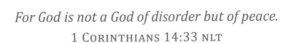
Thank You, Father, for hearing my prayers. *Amen.*

For God is not a God of disorder but of peace.
1 CORINTHIANS 14:33 NLT

DATE:

Dear Heavenly Father,

Today I am stressed because. . .

(and I'm giving it all to You!)

I'm feeling. . .

344

I need Your help focusing my thoughts on. . .

instead of

I need Your guidance with. . .

Help me to be thankful for all of life's blessings (big and small!), including. . .

Thank You, Father, for hearing my prayers. *Amen.*

Let us also lay aside every weight. . .looking to Jesus, the founder and perfecter of our faith.
HEBREWS 12:1–2 ESV

Dear Heavenly Father,
....
....
....
....
....

Today I am stressed because. . .
....
....
....
....
....
....
....
....
....
....
....

(and I'm giving it all to You!)

I'm feeling. . .
....
....
....
....
....
....
....
....
....
....
....
....
....
....

I need Your help focusing my thoughts on. . .

instead of

I need Your guidance with. . .

Help me to be thankful for all of life's blessings (big and small!), including. . .

Thank You, Father, for hearing my prayers. *Amen.*

"When someone gives you a hard time, respond with the supple moves of prayer, for then you are working out of your true selves, your God-created selves."
MATTHEW 5:44–45 MSG

DATE:

Dear Heavenly Father, ...
....
....
....
....
....

Today I am stressed because. . .
....
....
....
....
....
....
....
....
....
....
....

(and I'm giving it all to You!)

I'm feeling. . .
....
....
....
....
....
....
....
....
....
....
....
....
....
....

I need Your help focusing my thoughts on. . .

instead of

I need Your guidance with. . .

Help me to be thankful for all of life's blessings (big and small!), including. . .

Stand by the roads and look; and ask for the eternal paths, where the good, old way is; then walk in it, and you will find rest for your souls.
JEREMIAH 6:16 AMPC

DATE:

Dear Heavenly Father, ...
....
....
....
....
....

Today I am stressed because. . .
....
....
....
....
....
....
....
....
....
....

(and I'm giving it all to You!)

I'm feeling. . .
....
....
....
....
....
....
....
....
....
....
....
....
....

350

I need Your help focusing my thoughts on. . .

....

....

instead of

....

....

I need Your guidance with. . . ....

....

....

....

....

Help me to be thankful for all of life's blessings (big and small!), including. . .

....

....

....

....

....

Thank You, Father, for hearing my prayers. *Amen.*

Let the words of my mouth and the meditation of my heart be acceptable in Your sight, O Lord, my [firm, impenetrable] Rock and my Redeemer.
PSALM 19:14 AMPC

DATE:

Dear Heavenly Father,

Today I am stressed because. . .

(and I'm giving it all to You!)

I'm feeling. . .

I need Your help focusing my thoughts on. . .

_____

instead of

_____

_____

I need Your guidance with. . .

_____

_____

_____

_____

Help me to be thankful for all of life's blessings (big and small!), including. . .

_____

_____

_____

_____

Thank You, Father, for hearing my prayers. *Amen.*

Right behind you a voice will say,
"This is the way you should go,"
whether to the right or to the left.
Isaiah 30:21 nlt

DATE:

Dear Heavenly Father,
....
....
....
....
....
....

Today I am stressed because. . .
....
....
....
....
....
....
....
....
....
....
....

(and I'm giving it all to You!)

I'm feeling. . .
....
....
....
....
....
....
....
....
....
....
....
....
....
....
....
....

I need Your help focusing my thoughts on. . .

....

....

instead of

....

....

I need Your guidance with. . .

....

....

....

....

Help me to be thankful for all of life's
blessings (big and small!), including. . .

....

....

....

....

Thank You, Father, for hearing my prayers. *Amen.*

*The LORD replied, "I will personally go
with you. . .and I will give you rest—
everything will be fine for you."*
EXODUS 33:14 NLT

DATE:

Dear Heavenly Father,

Today I am stressed because. . .

(and I'm giving it all to You!)

I'm feeling. . .

356

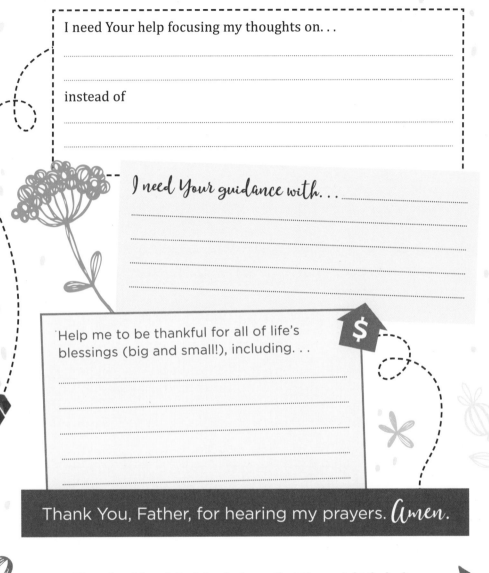

I need Your help focusing my thoughts on. . .

....

....

instead of

....

....

I need Your guidance with. . .

....

....

....

....

Help me to be thankful for all of life's blessings (big and small!), including. . .

....

....

....

....

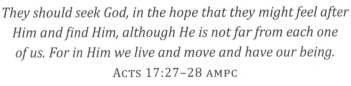

Thank You, Father, for hearing my prayers. *Amen.*

They should seek God, in the hope that they might feel after Him and find Him, although He is not far from each one of us. For in Him we live and move and have our being.
ACTS 17:27–28 AMPC

DATE:

Dear Heavenly Father, ...
....
....
....
....
....

Today I am stressed because. . .
....
....
....
....
....
....
....
....
....
....
....

(and I'm giving it all to You!)

I'm feeling. . .
....
....
....
....
....
....
....
....
....
....
....
....
....
....
....

I need Your help focusing my thoughts on. . .

....

....

instead of

....

....

I need Your guidance with. . . ....

....

....

....

....

Help me to be thankful for all of life's
blessings (big and small!), including. . .

....

....

....

....

Thank You, Father, for hearing my prayers. *Amen.*

I give you thanks, O Lord, with my whole heart. . . .
On the day I called, you answered me;
my strength of soul you increased.
PSALM 138:1, 3 ESV

DATE:

Dear Heavenly Father,

Today I am stressed because. . .

(and I'm giving it all to You!)

I'm feeling. . .

360

I need Your help focusing my thoughts on. . .

....

....

instead of

....

....

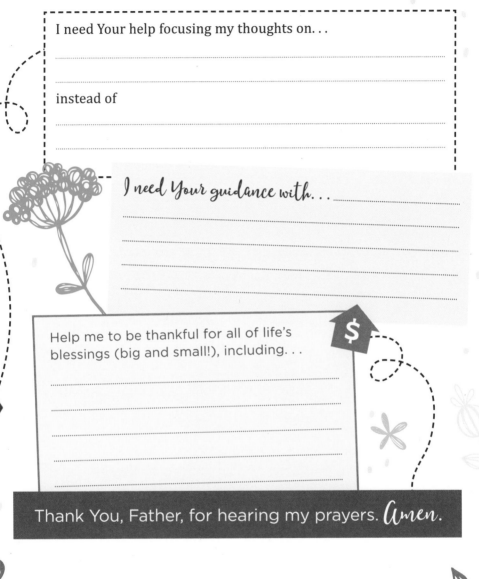

I need Your guidance with. . .

....

....

....

....

Help me to be thankful for all of life's blessings (big and small!), including. . .

....

....

....

....

Thank You, Father, for hearing my prayers. *Amen.*

Now ask and keep on asking and you will receive, so that your joy (gladness, delight) may be full and complete.
JOHN 16:24 AMPC

DATE:

Dear Heavenly Father,

Today I am stressed because. . .

(and I'm giving it all to You!)

I'm feeling. . .

I need Your help focusing my thoughts on. . .

_____

_____

instead of

_____

_____

I need Your guidance with. . .

_____

_____

_____

_____

Help me to be thankful for all of life's blessings (big and small!), including. . .

_____

_____

_____

_____

Thank You, Father, for hearing my prayers. *Amen.*

Be careful how you live. . . . Make the most of every opportunity. . . . Don't act thoughtlessly, but understand what the Lord wants you to do. . . . Be filled with the Holy Spirit. . .making music to the Lord in your hearts.
EPHESIANS 5:15–19 NLT

DATE:

Dear Heavenly Father,

Today I am stressed because. . .

(and I'm giving it all to You!)

I'm feeling. . .

I need Your help focusing my thoughts on. . .

instead of

I need Your guidance with. . .

Help me to be thankful for all of life's
blessings (big and small!), including. . .

Thank You, Father, for hearing my prayers. *Amen.*

*"Come to me. Get away with me and you'll recover
your life. I'll show you how to take a real rest.
Walk with me and work with me—watch how
I do it. Learn the unforced rhythms of grace."*
MATTHEW 11:28–30 MSG

DATE:

Dear Heavenly Father,

Today I am stressed because. . .

(and I'm giving it all to You!)

I'm feeling. . .

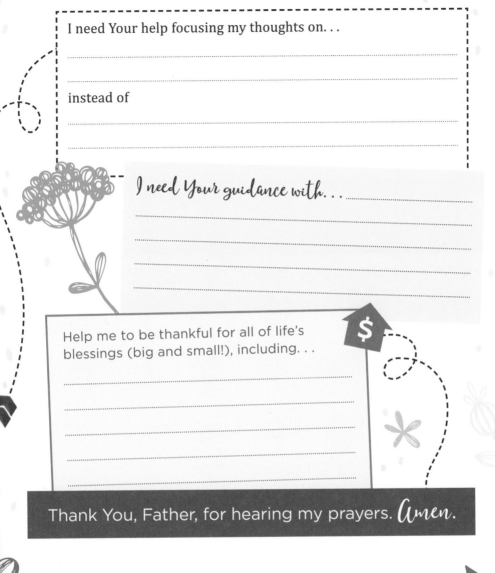

I need Your help focusing my thoughts on. . .

....

....

instead of

....

....

I need Your guidance with. . . ..

....

....

....

....

Help me to be thankful for all of life's blessings (big and small!), including. . .

....

....

....

....

....

Thank You, Father, for hearing my prayers. *Amen.*

In peace I will both lie down and sleep, for You, Lord,
alone make me dwell in safety and confident trust.
PSALM 4:8 AMPC

DATE:

Dear Heavenly Father,

Today I am stressed because. . .

(and I'm giving it all to You!)

I'm feeling. . .

I need Your help focusing my thoughts on. . .

instead of

I need Your guidance with. . .

Help me to be thankful for all of life's blessings (big and small!), including. . .

Thank You, Father, for hearing my prayers. *Amen.*

Sing God a brand-new song! Earth and everyone in it, sing! Sing to God—worship God!
PSALM 96:1–2 MSG

DATE:

Dear Heavenly Father,

Today I am stressed because...

(and I'm giving it all to You!)

I'm feeling...

I need Your help focusing my thoughts on. . .

....

....

instead of

....

....

I need Your guidance with. . . ....

....

....

....

....

Help me to be thankful for all of life's blessings (big and small!), including. . .

....

....

....

....

....

Thank You, Father, for hearing my prayers. *Amen.*

*Trust (lean on, rely on, and be confident) in the Lord
and do good; so shall you dwell in the land and feed
surely on His faithfulness, and truly you shall be fed.*
Psalm 37:3 ampc

DATE:

Dear Heavenly Father, ...
....
....
....
....
....

Today I am stressed because. . .
....
....
....
....
....
....
....
....
....

(and I'm giving it all to You!)

I'm feeling. . .
....
....
....
....
....
....
....
....
....
....
....
....
....

I need Your help focusing my thoughts on. . .

....

....

instead of

....

....

I need Your guidance with. . .

....

....

....

....

Help me to be thankful for all of life's blessings (big and small!), including. . .

....

....

....

....

Thank You, Father, for hearing my prayers. *Amen.*

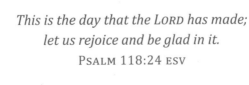

This is the day that the Lord has made;
let us rejoice and be glad in it.
Psalm 118:24 esv

DATE:

Dear Heavenly Father,

Today I am stressed because. . .

(and I'm giving it all to You!)

I'm feeling. . .

I need Your help focusing my thoughts on. . .

....

....

instead of

....

....

I need Your guidance with. . . ..

....

....

....

....

Help me to be thankful for all of life's
blessings (big and small!), including. . .

....

....

....

....

Thank You, Father, for hearing my prayers. *Amen.*

We're depending on GOD; he's everything we need.
What's more, our hearts brim with joy since we've
taken for our own his holy name. Love us, GOD,
with all you've got—that's what we're depending on.
PSALM 33:20–22 MSG

DATE:

Dear Heavenly Father,

Today I am stressed because. . .

(and I'm giving it all to You!)

I'm feeling. . .

I need Your help focusing my thoughts on. . .

_____

_____

instead of

_____

_____

I need Your guidance with. . . _____

_____

_____

_____

_____

Help me to be thankful for all of life's blessings (big and small!), including. . .

_____

_____

_____

_____

Thank You, Father, for hearing my prayers. *Amen.*

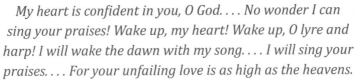

My heart is confident in you, O God. . . . No wonder I can sing your praises! Wake up, my heart! Wake up, O lyre and harp! I will wake the dawn with my song. . . . I will sing your praises. . . . For your unfailing love is as high as the heavens.
PSALM 57:7–10 NLT

DATE:

Dear Heavenly Father,

Today I am stressed because...

(and I'm giving it all to You!)

I'm feeling...

I need Your help focusing my thoughts on. . .

....

....

instead of

....

....

I need Your guidance with. . . ..

....

....

....

....

Help me to be thankful for all of life's blessings (big and small!), including. . .

....

....

....

....

....

Thank You, Father, for hearing my prayers. *Amen.*

I have learned to be content, whatever the circumstances may be. I know now how to live when things are difficult and I know how to live when things are prosperous. In general and in particular I have learned the secret of facing either poverty or plenty.
PHILIPPIANS 4:11–12 PHILLIPS

DATE:

Dear Heavenly Father,

Today I am stressed because. . .

(and I'm giving it all to You!)

I'm feeling. . .

I need Your help focusing my thoughts on. . .

....

....

instead of

....

....

I need Your guidance with. . .

....

....

....

....

Help me to be thankful for all of life's blessings (big and small!), including. . .

....

....

....

....

Thank You, Father, for hearing my prayers. *Amen.*

For his unfailing love toward those who fear him is as great as the height of the heavens above the earth. He has removed our sins as far from us as the east is from the west.
PSALM 103:11–12 NLT

DATE:

Dear Heavenly Father, ...
....
....
....
....
....

Today I am stressed because. . .
....
....
....
....
....
....
....
....
....
....
....

(and I'm giving it all to You!)

I'm feeling. . .
....
....
....
....
....
....
....
....
....
....
....
....
....
....
....
....

I need Your help focusing my thoughts on. . .

....

....

instead of

....

....

I need Your guidance with. . .

....

....

....

....

Help me to be thankful for all of life's
blessings (big and small!), including. . .

....

....

....

....

....

Thank You, Father, for hearing my prayers. *Amen.*

*He's already made it plain how to live, what to do, what GOD
is looking for. . . . It's quite simple: Do what is fair and just
to your neighbor, be compassionate and loyal in your love,
and don't take yourself too seriously—take God seriously.*
MICAH 6:8 MSG

Check Out These Faith Maps for the Entire Family. . .

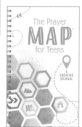

The Prayer Map for Men
978-1-64352-438-2

The Prayer Map for Women
978-1-63609-763-3
978-1-63609-762-6

The Prayer Map for Girls
978-1-68322-559-1

The Prayer Map for Boys
978-1-68322-558-4

The Prayer Map for Teens
978-1-68322-556-0

These purposeful prayer journals are a fun and creative way to more fully experience the power of prayer. Each page guides you to write out thoughts, ideas, and lists. . .which then creates a specific "map" for you to follow as you talk to God. Each map includes a spot to record the date, so you can look back on your prayers and see how God has worked in your life. *The Prayer Map* will not only encourage you to spend time talking with God about the things that matter most. . .it will also help you build a healthy spiritual habit of continual prayer for life!